what i couldn't see before

God's Not Holding Out on You,
He's Holding on to You

Linsey Shields
Foreword by John Stickl

© 2024 by Linsey Shields

All rights reserved. No part of this book may be reproduced or transmitted in any form or by any means, electronic or mechanical, including photography and recording, or by any information storage or retrieval system, except as may be expressly permitted in writing by the publisher. The only exception is brief quotations in printed reviews.

All Scripture quotations, unless otherwise indicated, are taken from the Holy Bible, New International Version®, NIV®. Copyright ©1973, 1978, 1984, 2011 by Biblica, Inc.™ Used by permission of Zondervan. All rights reserved worldwide. www.zondervan.com The "NIV" and "New International Version" are trademarks registered in the United States Patent and Trademark Office by Biblica, Inc.™

Cover by Dylan McDuffie

Purposed Publishing

Published by Purposed Publishing
www.purposedpublishing.com

ISBN: 979-8-9915395-2-4 (paperback)
ISBN: 979-8-9915395-3-1 (hardback)

Endorsements

In What I Couldn't See Before, Linsey courageously shares her most private battles for our benefit. She takes her readers on a journey through valleys of desperation and hilltops of hope to discover a core truth: we may each have our own difficulties in life, but we never walk alone.

Pastor Becca Reynolds
Executive Pastor at Valley Creek Church

The author's openness about her own personal story of wrestling with God's goodness and love in the midst of brokenness, pain and suffering will allow others to resonate and be encouraged as they walk their own journey. Her compassion and gentleness is palpable and you will feel as if she is sitting with you on your couch, sharing heartfelt truth of how Jesus met her in the midst of her pain and never let go. She opens up and shares with raw vulnerability how she came to see purpose in the pain and that God absolutely was not holding out on her, but was indeed holding on to her.

Linda Mason, LMFTS
Koinonia Christian Counseling

To Rob, who has shown me the consistent love of Jesus. You have patiently loved me when I didn't even know how to love myself. We have walked through the valleys, and we are both stronger for it. We're better together, and our best days are ahead!

To our kids, you have been my mat carriers. You have your own journey in all of this. I pray that as you keep going, you go with Jesus, knowing He is good and good to you. You are unbelievably loved, courageous, wise, funny and compassionate. I love that you made me a mom. You were made to move mountains, and I pray y'all move them together.

To the reader, our brokenness leads to breakthrough and here's to you finding yours.

"The Lord is not slow in keeping his promise, as some understand slowness. Instead he is patient with you, not wanting anyone to perish, but everyone to come to repentance."

2 Peter 3:9

"Jesus replied, "You do not realize now what I am doing, but later you will understand.""

John 13:7

Foreword

Hope. The confident expectation of the goodness of God. While there are many things in life that we can live without, hope is not one of them. Humanity was created to live in the heavenly atmosphere of hope. Like water to our body or air to our lungs, hope is vital to our soul – vital to having a healthy soul. Hope is the active ingredient in a life of faith that keeps us moving forward regardless of the headwinds we may face. But like most of the important things in life, hope is often stolen, killed, or destroyed as we journey along the way. Hope, while it may start out seemingly strong in our lives, can quickly become replaced by "This is as good as it gets." "My best days are behind me." "Things will never change." "My life will always be this way." Before we know it, hope gets replaced by despair and we start to live with the confident expectation of bad.

However, we must remember the words of Jesus when he said, "In this world you will have trouble. But take heart! I have overcome the world" (John 16:33). In other words, Jesus says in this life there will be trials, hardships, sufferings, brokenness, situations and circumstances that we would rather avoid. But in the midst of the disappointments, His goodness is always at hand and within reach, even when we can't see it – especially when we can't see it. This is why Jesus' main message was "Repent, for the Kingdom of heaven is at hand" (Matthew 4:17). Change your mind, hope is here! Jesus is reminding us that hope is not a feeling, an emotion, or wishful thinking, but rather hope is a person and His name is Jesus. That in the midst of the difficulties, Living Hope is always among us. His goodness is leading us, working in us, and following us all the days of our lives – of this we can be confident. In many ways, hope is simply about perspective. Am I focusing on the right thing? The invitation to "take heart" is to simply learn to look at my circumstances through Jesus instead of looking at Jesus through my circumstances. Since hope has already been resurrected from the dead it cannot die, we just tend to lose sight of it. It is all too easy to over-focus on the problem of pain instead of the Person called Living Hope.

One of the greatest ways we keep hope in front of us is by learning from other people's journeys. As we watch others running their race holding on to hope in the midst of despair, it helps us take ahold of hope in our disappointments. That is why *What I Couldn't See Before* is so powerful. Over the past few decades, I have had a front row seat to Linsey's life. She has endured trials and hardships that would have left most people bitter and offended. However, Linsey hasn't just survived her difficulties, she has thrived through them. She has held onto Living Hope in a way that has allowed her to run her race with joy, a race that is now inspiring others. Her life story gives us a vision of who we can become, a hope carrier, in the midst of our disappointments. I believe her story is a testimony of the goodness of God that will lift your head and change your perspective from looking at Jesus through your circumstances to looking at your circumstances through Jesus.

Linsey Shields

It's only through the Living Hope that we can live a life of hope. May you start to see his goodness all around you even if you couldn't see it before.

John Stickl
Lead Pastor Valley Creek Church
Author of *Follow the Cloud*

Table of Contents

Endorsements iii

Foreword vii

Introduction 1

Chapter One: Half Naked, Fully Exposed 5

Chapter Two: Peek Behind the Curtain of Pain 19

Chapter Three: Don't Sleep with Shame 33

Chapter Four: Courage Over Comfort 45

Chapter Five: Trust the Process 61

Chapter Six: Grappling with Grace 75

Chapter Seven: Hilltops and Valleys 91

Chapter Eight: Paralyzed by Panic 107

Chapter Nine: Don't Fold on Your Faith 125

Chapter Ten: Humility in Hardship 139

Chapter Eleven: Run your Race 153

Acknowledgments 181

Introduction

Friend, have you struggled to see God moving in your life? Do you sometimes doubt God is good? Have you given up on Him because you're certain He's given up on you? Or, did you deviate from God, and now you feel discarded by Him?

The world will tell us that we don't need God.

But then, we find ourselves in need of God.

Me too, friend. I've settled in a season or two, of not thinking I needed, nor honestly wanted God. Only, the indulgence ended.

Circumstances smacked me in the face, but then so did Grace! His forgiveness was unfathomable.

I'm here to tell you that the world eventually dries out with desire, God never left, and His grace shows up in unexpected ways.

Likewise, God doesn't put you in time out for turning away. Your pain isn't punishment, and He hasn't turned His back on you.

Our brokenness leads to breakthrough, and I've certainly had my share of both.

Now, I not only need God, but I want Him in my life more than anything. I pray you find Hope in these pages. I have found freedom and victory but not without hovering heartache. So, what do you say, let's envision a cozy cafe. I have my americano with a splash of oat milk & you enjoy your crafted creation. I share this with you, in the center of your chaos, to say "You can do hard things."

This is a story of learning to trust God, healing, but also the root of why I needed healing. Unpacking the story is essential to understanding it.

"And they overcame him by the blood of the Lamb, and by the word of their testimony..."[1]

Our testimony, the recounting of our sorrows, struggles & strongholds & how the blood of the Lamb came to save us - it ALL overcomes the enemy.

Our stories are our sword. And, when we tell our tale, it helps others find the courage to pick up their sword, to own their story with Jesus. My story contains faith, wrestle, surrender, excruciating pain, and the loss of life but not how you'd think. Yet, God brings dead things to life. And, let's not forget about HOPE. "And hope does not put us to shame, because God's love has been poured out into our hearts through the Holy Spirit, who has been given to us."[2]

Now, I stand, waving my sword in the air, certain that Satan doesn't win this story. And, I'm here to plea, don't let him win yours.

This is for the believer that has sought God with all their heart, pursued healing because their life depended on it and begged for mercy, only to be left empty handed, no answers nor healing. For you, that's on your last drop of hope, the one that wearily waves your white flag, desperate for this to end, I see you. God sees you in your suffering. To you, that can't conceive or your marriage is mangled. You, that feels this is somehow your fault. He sees you.

---

[1] Revelation 12:11
[2] Romans 5:5

You, that feels like you've done everything right and still nothing. To you, that's smothered in shame, paralyzed by your past, He sees you. He loves you, and He forgives you. To you, that's buried in bills from your relentless pursuit to stop the pain. You, where others don't believe you and to you, that doesn't believe God. You, that's still sick with a broken heart or a broken body. You, that miscarried. You, that's seen All the doctors, done all the diets and none offer hope, He sees you. You, that feels it will always be this way, this will never get better. You, that feels abandoned by God and that He's the villain in your story, He sees you.

You, you were told your intercession would find fruition, but you're as desolate as the desert, He sees you.

You are not alone.

I'm charging into the enemy's territory to shield and deflect Satan's strategy on your soul. You see, the battle isn't out there, it always starts in here, where our souls silently scream.

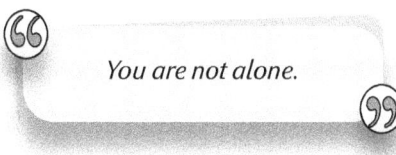

You are not alone.

"The human spirit can endure in sickness, but a crushed spirit who can bear?"[3]

Our scars tell a story, and here is mine...what I couldn't see before.

---

[3] Proverbs 18:14

Chapter One

Half Naked, Fully Exposed

Here I was again, half naked but fully exposed. Lamentably, this was familiar territory. I laid on the frigid, sterile table as the nurse prepared me for yet another procedure. The lights, so ghastly, they were almost blinding. The nurse bid me adieu. The tears dropped to the table like a dripping faucet when it's freezing. Why do we let the faucet drip? To keep the pipe from bursting. Well, I was icy and isolated, and I could have burst at any moment. I was left alone with my thoughts.

How did I get here? I'm a burden! I'm far too young. Everyone in the lobby has silver hair and wheelchairs. Rob didn't sign up for this. Neither did my kids. For cryin' out loud, neither did I! My flesh was fragile in every sense of the word.

The doctor came in to do his thing. Only this time, he continued to painstakingly bump my bone while trying to locate the precise point to inject. Mind you, I had to be as still as a statue the entire time. Some choose anesthesia for this procedure, but we opted out. We had kids at home. Rob had a job to go to. Life carried on. We wanted life to go on. We Needed life to go on. We were thirsty for normalcy. So, I laid there, wide awake but lifeless.

This doctor had successfully alleviated my pain many times before. So much so, that I wanted to ask if they offered a punch card for these procedures, and your 10th one is free or something.

Surely, there was a perk for the pain somewhere. I digress, the doctor was struggling to insert due to copious amounts of inflammation. The tears continued to trickle while four-letter words wanted to spew. Silent suffering took on a whole new meaning in that space. The agony was awful! Doc finally injected, and now I was locked and loaded…until next time. As he exited, I was told I could pull my pants up. But, my pride was left on the floor. All dignity was lost and THEN, I had to be wheel-chaired out per protocol. Salt to the wound, people, salt to the wound.

Have you ever found yourself in the most unforeseen circumstances? And yet, here you are, again. Feeling broken beyond repair. Feeling alone and wondering if the situation will ever straighten out. My heart goes out to all of you that are inaudibly afflicted. The empty womb but a full heart, ready to love. The one that sleeps next to a stranger and longs for connection. The one that lives with perpetual, physical pain and you've learned to pose and pretend. The one that has tangled thoughts and anguishing anxiety but your makeup is your mask. As you wearily wade through your pain, Jesus says, "You do not realize now what I am doing, but later you will understand."[4]

While we wait for Jesus to move, our desires dim and our waiting wanes. We begin to question His goodness. These doubts were beginning to lurk, linger & dilute my disposition.

As mentioned, I had been a repeat recipient of this doctor's services. And, by the grace of God and His kindness, the injections sustained me far longer than subscribed. There were numerous days that we savored in those years of sustenance. But, the duration between shots was thinning, just like the lining of my joint. I feared this option was becoming obsolete. Then, the doctor confirmed my suspicion. This method to pacify my pangs was ceasing. Doc then said, with as much tenderness that he could create, "I can no longer help you after this one. Its' time for you to consider what you've postponed. You'll need to prepare for the inevitable."

No words. Rob and I had no words on the drive home. Instead, we chose to ride the waves of our momentary mitigation for as long as we could, hoping this moment would last for months.

We put a band aid on our brokenness.

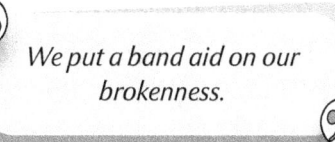
We put a band aid on our brokenness.

Life carried on. This reprieve gave us much to be thankful for: family strolls in the evenings and ousting my kids at knockout in basketball in the driveway. I no longer was driving without abrupt

---
[4] John 13:7

stops to exit the car and ease the excruciating pain. I could sit at meals and mosey without being bolstered from our booth because the pain was too piercing. I had the ability to snuggle and squeeze my kids unrestrictedly. We lingered in laughter, and I had the mental, emotional and physical capacity to just be present with my people. All too often, when pain is your portion, your focus is foggy. Much of my energy was devoted to surviving the day, not thriving. Chronic illness left me feeling lifeless some days, a shell of a frame forcing one foot in front of the other. Consequently, in the superb streaks, I felt I could conquer the world. I was able to live life to the full and gain a rooted recognition for the under-appreciated blessings in our life. We were grateful for the good days, but we also grieved the prescribed procedure with an unknown and unwanted arrival. It was a race against time. This injection hung in there for ten far-fetched months.

Before long, sleep returned to being a thing of the past. I could no longer stand lying in bed with my husband. The pain was successful at stealing my slumber. Uncomfortable was the only position I knew, and I couldn't bear the thought of preventing Rob from sleeping, too. So, I limped into the living room each night, pillow under one arm with an ice pack in the other hand. "I love you honey" were the words we exchanged in the dark. I made my way to the recliner, my body desperate to relax.

I would occasionally read or journal but mostly, I talked to God. I cried to God. I pleaded with God. "God, I believe! Help me with my unbelief!" I begged for Him to take away the pain, to heal my body. I'd recite His Word back to Him, the promises He states, "and by His wounds we are healed."[5]

---

[5] Isaiah 53:5

"He will never leave you nor forsake you."[6]

The fact was: I needed a hip replacement because rheumatoid arthritis had robbed me and destroyed the lining of my joint. The truth was: I believed that God was the God of miracles, that He could do the impossible, that He could heal my hip in haste. I didn't need a physician to fix me, I was on the Home team of my Heavenly Healer. So, for a couple of months, I bemoaned the soundtrack of my suffering to the Lord, in the dark of night. The lyrics changed some, but for the most part, my request was on repeat, night after night. All the while, my sobbing stayed silent to avoid waking any of my people. Yes, one could point out the kindness of God to have sustained me to that point. But, I just couldn't get over my fortune when I wasn't even forty. Old people get hip replacements, jokes are made about hip replacements, they weren't for young moms like me. So, I kept beseeching the Father to tame my torment.

And then one day, something shifted. (Now, at this point, we'd all love to read that I rose from my recliner and ran to wake Rob, fully healed and pain free.) We long for the happy endings, right? We're desperate for God to get the glory for our story, and we're convinced there's only one storyline for that to happen. We forget God's sovereignty in moments like these, His total control of His creation.

My theology had been tested, and my faith was fractured and on the floor. Friends, I'm married to a pastor. Can I say that out loud? These were dark times indeed. I felt brokenhearted BY God. I told my dear husband that I was done asking God for help. I proceeded to ask Rob that if I was hurting, I cried out to him for

---

[6] Deuteronomy 31:6

help incessantly, and he continually did not come to my aid, should I keep asking for help or move on? He got my point. Right or wrong, I felt betrayed BY God, like my prayers fell on deaf ears. How on earth could a Good Father not run to rescue His child crying out?! We were now thirteen years into my rheumatoid arthritis journey. As leaders in the church, we had prayed for and witnessed others' repeatedly receiving their miracles. It's not that we felt we deserved it, but we believed He could do it. But He didn't. He hadn't. My trust was tattered and torn. I went quiet with God. He, seemingly, had gone quiet on me so I thought I'd reciprocate. I was hurting and felt deeply, deeply wounded by the One I had asked to heal my wounds.

As a 1 (Moral Reformer) on the enneagram, all was not right in my world, so I withdrew to a four (like us 1's do in stress,) and I became isolated, quiet, independent and introspective. (The enneagram is simply a personality theory/tool comprised of nine different numbers, and each number has a different motivator, desire, fear and also inherent struggle. This tool is just that, a tool, not the Gospel. But, it can provide a lot of clarity, self-awareness, understanding and compassion for both yourself and others. Each person has one primary number they identify with and that number goes to a different number in stress and yet another number in health. It sounds overwhelming and complicated, but it's really not.

I wasn't opposed to approaching God on behalf of others, but that's as far as I went with it. It felt far too risky to open my heart up again. I was hanging onto Hope that God is good, but I had resolved that He wasn't good to me nor that He loved me. I guessed I wasn't worthy of His goodness. Since transparency is the theme here, I confess that I began to feel betrayed by Rob, too. Each day, He'd go to work (our church,) petition for others, serve others, all in the name of Jesus. It was like Rob was on God's team and I was the kid no one ever picked for theirs. The enemy was stirring the pot.

As Satan would have it, shame seeped in. Deceit was dragging me back to the depths. "You know this is your fault, right?" "You caused this."

I didn't have the energy to fight it, so I believed it.

Has the great Accuser been accusing you? Do you feel you're to blame for your lack of breakthrough? We become so desperate for healing: our marriage, our finances, our health, our children, that we lose sight of the Healer. Friend, you are not alone. And, the Foe is not your friend. While our adversary chirps and chants, our faith can begin to crumble.

We lose confidence in our Creator when pain is the narrator.

My grit was grinding down to granules. I lacked the fortitude to keep fighting. And maybe, that was a good thing. I had wrestled with God until I was weary. Jacob wrestled with God, but his blessing came after just one night of contending. We were over a decade into this. I wanted to have Jacob's resolve and refuse to quit until God blessed me. I wanted to overcome the struggle. I wanted to see God face to face. Jacob was left with a glorious limp (because of his hip) and a new name.[7] I'd settle for a glorious limp, but God, please take away the pain.

As we trudged along, I crossed paths with two women I didn't do life with on a regular basis. I actually hadn't even met one of them until an intersection at church one night. At this time, our church offered Thursday night services. The whole family attended this night together. My husband was temporarily serving at one of our other campuses on the weekends, so we weren't typically together for worship. After service, he was in "chit-chat traffic" as our son coined the phrase. I, honestly, was going through the motions. I had picked our youngest up from his kids' service, and we were working our way to the door. I preferred to remain unseen in my distress. Rob stopped me and wanted me to meet the couple he was chatting with. They didn't attend on Thursdays consistently, either. God works that way sometimes, right? One thing led to another, and somewhere in there it was shared that I was gluten free. She proceeded to ask me why. I explained that eating a gluten free diet helped my inflammation with RA. She then so directly said "You can be free from that, you know!"

A thousand thoughts clashed in my head, and I quickly reminded my face to not expose my heart.

Over the years, we had to learn to guard our hearts and give grace to others. There are so many well-intentioned people that want to help. "Have you tried this?" "You should do that." "This helped us." "I recently heard about this new method."

You get what I'm saying. I'd learned to filter feedback with the Holy Spirit's guidance. If I was supposed to hear their help, please

---

[7] Genesis 32:24-32

let me. If not, may it fall on deaf ears and off of me so that I don't absorb it as shame or something I'm not doing that I should be, in order to obtain freedom.

Soooo, I quickly primed myself for her proposal. "Here we go. I wonder what she has for me that I haven't already heard. Smile Linsey. Nod Linsey. Lay it on me, and may it stick if there's Truth in there somewhere." She asked if I was a reader. I concurred. She then told me that she was going to give Rob a book for me to read that Sunday. I hadn't the slightest idea of what was stirring.

This same week, a friend (a wife to one of our elders) saw me and knew enough of my story to know I was hurting, both physically and spiritually…really in every way. She encouraged me to reach out to their chiropractor. She prefaced that he had a non-traditional approach when I showed her my look of skepticism. I had been to a chiropractor years prior for this issue. I frequented there so many times that I definitely deserved some loyalty points or something. I went far too long out of desperation, and I felt he had taken advantage of us financially, knowing how frenzied we were for a remedy. I begrudgingly agreed to call said chiropractor, but I confessed to her how very jaded I was, without expectations, depleted, running on E with hope, hard-hearted by hurt. She didn't judge me at that moment. I bared my soul, and I didn't spook her away.

We all need people like this in our lives. You know, a friend you don't have to fix your face for. Do you have that friend? I have Godly relationships that I met with consistently, every week at a local coffee shop for years, even leading up to this. We need those that we can come to the table with, empty-handed and absolutely nothing to offer but a crushed spirit. I certainly came to the table with no words during this time. I remember showing up a couple of times when I was at my lowest, and I honestly just sat there and cried. We all sat in that sacred space and grieved silently. They didn't try to make it better, they just sat with me in the weight of it all. I really don't think they had words, either. And, that's ok. This reminds me of Job and his people Before they missed the mark in being his friend. "Then they sat on the ground with him for seven days and seven nights. No one said a word to him, because they saw how great his suffering was."[8]

Sometimes, silence is all that needs to be said. Presence is powerful at times like these. "Rejoice with those who rejoice; mourn with those who mourn."[9]

> Sometimes, silence is all that needs to be said.

We all need people that love Jesus and are safe enough where we can say out loud, "I can't even muster a mustard seed of faith." To not shame us. To not stamp us with some trite "God won't give you more than you can handle" utterance and then move on. To place courage in us. To see us in our suffering. To love us when we have no love to give, or even when we're convinced we're unlovable. To listen. To learn. Challenge, yes, but may I beg of you to only do so with the Holy Spirit's solicitation. I'm saddened by stories of good-intentioned people in or out of the church that have wreaked more havoc than helped.

If you have been on the receiving end of this, please hold this hug I'm sending your way. I am so very sorry for the hurt on the other side of people's words. I remember one time in particular

---

[8] Job 2:13
[9] Romans 12:15

when a lady in the atrium at church asked me how I was feeling. She then proceeded to tell me I looked like death. Not sick, not hurting, not sad. Death. That's all she said. She cut me to my core. What she didn't know is that I was already wrestling with the fear that the pain just might take me down. I had to call a friend that afternoon to come sit with me while my kiddos napped. I needed her to hold my hurt, let me lament and have her pray and speak Truth over me. That comment cemented.

Friends, our words are weighty. For good or bad. If you've meant well but it landed wrong, God's grace abounds. I have been guilty of this, too. Situations of suffering require us to be slow to speak and quick to listen. And, if we speak preemptively, a sincere apology can go a long way. Remember, silence speaks volumes in scenarios like these.

Let's revert back…a book was headed my way and I had an appointment with a chiropractor. Two seemingly humdrum developments. God seemed segregated and quiet. I figured if He wasn't listening to me, and I couldn't hear Him, then maybe He would speak through others. I was on the brink of breakthrough but hanging on by a hair.

CHAPTER ONE REFLECTIONS

1. "You do not realize now what I am doing, but later you will understand." John 13:7

   What circumstances have you found yourself in where you're questioning or have questioned the goodness of God?

   _____
   _____
   _____
   _____

2. "Consider it pure joy, my brothers and sisters, whenever you face trials of many kinds, because you know that the testing of your faith produces perseverance." James 1:2-3

   How can enduring pain and suffering strengthen your faith and character?

   _____
   _____
   _____
   _____

3. "Be strong and take heart, all you who hope in the Lord." Psalm 31:24

   How do you maintain hope and trust in God when your prayers seem unanswered?

   _____
   _____
   _____
   _____

4. "Rejoice with those who rejoice; mourn with those who mourn." Romans 12:15

   Who do you know that is struggling in their circumstances? How can you be a source of comfort and support to them?

   _____
   _____
   _____
   _____

Chapter Two

Peek Behind the Curtain of Pain

While God felt far-removed, I was about to discover He was close-at-hand. I was on the cusp of peeking behind my curtain of adversity.

Sunday rolled around, and Rob rolled in from church, with the book…the questionable book the lady had mentioned a few days prior. I remember it being an unusually warm, December day.

We had plans to take the fam to the park and not let the beautiful day pass us by. But first, I wanted to see what this book was all about. I picked it up and perused the pages. The synopsis was about spiritual root to disease. I had never heard of such a thing. Curious, I thumbed my way to the index and found "rheumatoid arthritis." Completely unaware of what I was about to read, I made my way to the precise page. And then, what I read left me without words.

SELF-HATRED

The spiritual root of RA is self-hatred?! I could not believe my eyes. No words or even thoughts. I was stunned. What was I to do with what I just read? I was numb. We were still making our way to the park, but I told my husband that my mind was miles away. The kiddos swung, climbed and slid while I was lost in thought. I eventually managed to shelf the discovery and enjoy our family for the rest of the evening. The next morning though, I was scheduled to see the recommended chiropractor.

The day emerged. I dropped the kids off at school, and I made my way to my appointment. The Holy Spirit was undeniably present the minute I walked in. Worship music playing, oils diffusing, peace available, a friendly face at the front desk, but I'm not gonna lie, I was straight up skeptical. He called me back and asked me to take a seat wherever I felt comfortable. He had a nice sitting area, but I wanted to say, "Joke's on you, man. There's no seat in here that'll make me feel comfortable - emotionally or physically."

He asked me to share a bit of why I was there. I led with, "I'm here because a friend told me I should come, but I've been to chiropractors before. I don't trust them. I feel like my last one took advantage of me financially and saw me far longer than he was able to help. So, I'm hesitant to trust again."

I'm sure he was like, "Well, nice to meet you, too." I was guarded and cynical and he knew it. He told me he had two words that came to mind for me, but that he would share them at the end of our time. He also said he totally understood my hesitancy to hope he could help. I felt myself begin to soften a smidge. I explained that I had had RA since 2005. It was 2018 at the time. I shared that I was told I needed a hip and shoulder replacement years prior. I continued by sharing that the pain had returned in my hip and was unbearable. We talked some more, and our time came to a close. He hadn't even assessed me yet, or I suppose I should say he hadn't assessed me physically. He had most assuredly been assessing me. He told me he wasn't going to do any testing, etc. that session. He was respecting my apprehension. As we wrapped up, he circled back to the two words he had saved for the end. He proceeded to tell me that those words were: UNWORTHY and NOT GOOD ENOUGH.

Are you kidding me?! The weight of his words made me weep. The tears emerged with shackles of shame exposed. I was broken and bawling. I fell apart in front of this stranger. Between sobs, I explained the book and root I had just learned of for RA the night before. What was happening?

BIG side-note...When we were in a season of good health with my RA, God called us to adopt a little boy from China that was born without his right eye. He joined our family at the age of 2 in 2016. We had numerous "only God" confirmations all throughout that process. We clung tight to those when we were in China for sixteen days, and those confirmations continue to carry us through the hard today. I still remember the moment we met him like it was yesterday. He walked in with all he possessed on his person, unkempt, flushed cheeks and I whispered quietly, "I'm in love."

We made our way back to the hotel, and he and I got down to our bare necessities. We laid him on my chest, to have physical touch, to bond and build trust. That love would prove to be tough from the beginning, and God quickly reminded me that we are to love because of Whose he was, not for his behavior or lack thereof. Adoption sadly begins from brokenness. It's not God's original plan

What I Couldn't See Before

for family, but we knew we had been adopted into God's family. We knew that God places the lonely in families and that we've been adopted into Jesus's family. So, after much prayer, counsel and support, we added to our family via adoption. We went through intense training to prepare to help our child deal with his trauma that he would understandably bring with him. Experts said to grieve our losses before he came home with his. We were also told that the first six months to a year would be awful, to brace ourselves for the tumultuous tide. This was all to be expected with adoption. We had done our due diligence to prepare for his arrival.

And, I'll just say that the first year proved true to what we were told. But year two wasn't letting up, either.

I was the primary one with him all the time, and things just weren't getting better. So, I began to believe that I was the problem. If only I were (fill in the blank,) then things would have improved by now. I believed the lie that I was a horrible mom. I had been a stay-at-home mom for twelve years at that point, and I felt sure that I was failing at motherhood. If I wasn't a good mom, then what was I? I was in a dark place. Confiding in a counselor was helping, but we saw no relief in sight. We could not grasp why things were still so hard, so I gave way to the temptation that if I were more… (patient, nurturing, firm,…I don't know) things would ease up.

Fast forward to my chiropractor appointment, and we were well into our 2nd year of our adoption journey. I was bogged down by shame, and the chiropractor could see right through me.

The storm of that season had been a beatdown to my soul.

So, "unworthy" and "not good enough" rang loud and clear. Yep, the struggle was real. This guy was reading my mail. For clarity, he was not speaking harm over me. He simply shared the truth of what the Holy Spirit revealed to him during our brief time, with grace. I then opened up with how hard the last season had been with adoption and how confident I was that I was the problem.

He listened, he offered his presence and then he earned my trust with what he said next. "Jesus is doing some heart-work in you right now, and I don't want to get in His way. Why don't you come back and see me in six weeks."

What? You don't want me to come back three times a week for eight weeks and basically have our paycheck direct deposited to you?! Okay, this guy must be legit. He's different. He is clearly partnering with God in his work, he is Spirit-led.

I was spun up when I went in, and as I left, things began to unravel, for my good. I limped in there with a broken heart and fractured theology. I felt God was the heartbreaker. He wasn't answering my cries for relief from my physical pangs. I felt He had turned His back on me and betrayed me. He seemed quiet, and I was desolate. But. . . but, bit by bit, I began to see. God had been there all along. He never left as He promises He won't.

His Word says, "The Lord is near to the brokenhearted And saves those who are crushed in spirit. Many are the afflictions of the righteous, BUT the Lord delivers him out of them all."[10]

"It is the Lord who goes before you. He will be with you; He will not leave you or forsake you. Do not fear or be dismayed."[11]

I felt forsaken and definitely dismayed. So, what was happening now? The curtain was being pulled back. My eyes were being opened. God WAS with me in those dark nights. He WAS there.

---

[10] Psalm 34:18-19
[11] Deuteronomy 31:8

What I Couldn't See Before

He grieved alongside me as a good Parent does. Obviously, He knew the bigger picture while I was temporarily (albeit long) being tormented. He is a God of order, and He cared for my heart to be healed Before my body would be.

As parents, (teachers/mentors/coaches) it wounds us when our kids walk through heavy heartache. But, most times, we can see the fruit and freedom for them on the other side of their trial when they can't see it themselves. We have faith for them in the interim. And, we know, that if we swoop in and save them from that storm, (tempting as it may be) they won't experience the goodness and faithfulness of God on display to them. They won't have a marker-stone to look back on to say, "remember when."

All too often, we put God in a box. God, I know you can heal. I believe you can heal, and healing looks like this. That's what I expect, what I want, what I think is best. We confine Him to categories of healing, when instead, we need to say to heck with the box and God, do what only You can do. He can see under the hood when we can't.

Life had left me lifeless. My trust in God was the same.

Have you been there? Are you there now? When I no longer believed that He cared, I learned that He cared far more than I could fathom. Friend, He cares for you. Everything was surfacing. Self-hatred? Unworthy? Not good enough? I had believed those lies, too. I had been a friend of my foe for too long and believed the lies of the enemy. His trickery trapped. I had subconsciously sabotaged my soul and surmised that I was unworthy, undeserving of God's grace for So. Many. Years! Yes, Satan had been smothering me in shame during the arduous adoption journey, but this went WAY back. All the way back to high school. I suffered natural consequences from that circumstance, but I falsely believed All. That. Time. that it was my fault I had RA. I thought I was being punished for my poor choices from all those years ago. I thought I deserved RA. I hadn't held that theology for others but only myself. The lies had been exposed and brought to the light, and I was done with the darkness and deception.

I had a broken body and broken beliefs, but I did not cause RA.

Friend, what lie are you believing? Where do you feel ignored or forgotten? What chains are choking you? Are you discouraged in the dark of night? I wish I could comfort you and say I'm sorry. I'm so very sorry for your pain. I can now say with assurance that the God of the Universe doesn't withhold good from us nor does He want us to suffer.

I pray that God peels back the curtain on your pain, too and gives you a glimpse that He's been by your side through it all. I know that our hearts grow hoarse, and countless are the times we cry out to God for His holy help. We're desperate for Him to ease the anguish that stifles our soul.

"How long must I wrestle with my thoughts and day after day have sorrow in my heart? How long will my enemy triumph over me?"[12]

Friend, He knows. He sees you. I pray this book partners with you in your pain. You are not alone.

---

[12] Psalm 13:2

What I Couldn't See Before

A war is waged Every. Single. Day. for our hearts. We cannot forfeit our souls. God's word says, "The thief comes only to steal and kill and destroy; I have come that they may have life and have it to the full."[13]

The thief had done a lot of stealing and killing in my life, and I finally put my foot down. No more. I declare that over you today, as well.

The enemy no longer has authority.

My fingers are protesting. . .pain is often the very thing that draws us near to Him, to free us of the strongholds and false freedoms of this world. Pain, as painful as it is, can be a gift and a gate that leads to experiencing the fullness of God's grace (if we let it.) Abundance IS attainable. We must allow the Holy Spirit to prune our pain for a harvest that will reach far beyond our grief. I have learned that.

This pain wasn't punishment, it was an intimate invitation to set me free.

I had been mad at God. You have permission to be mad, too. He can handle our honesty, that's where the intimacy comes in. I felt abandoned, dismissed and

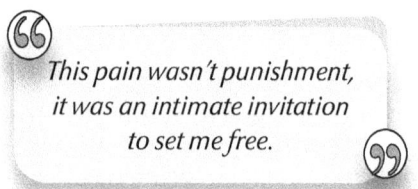

This pain wasn't punishment, it was an intimate invitation to set me free.

deeply, deeply wounded by God. I was done. Not done with God, but done asking. I obliged to "keep the faith". But for others, not

---
[13] John 10:10

myself. I still believed He was God but had decided to keep my distance. Trust was torn.

I doubted God's goodness. Did He love me? If He did, then why on earth would He ignore His child? I'd cried out in writhing agony, again and again in the darkest of nights. My soul was shattered, and my faith frayed. God felt anything But near to my broken heart.

We weren't created to desensitize and devalue our hearts and hurts. We're meant to thrive. Thrive? Yes! So, how do we live with our whole hearts when they feel anything but?

We bring our pain to Jesus. We don't run, stuff it, hide it or ignore it. We part with our woes and worries at the cross. "Cast all your cares on Him because He cares for you."[14]

We release our anger. Let Him hold us in the sorrow and silence. He grieves with us. "Yet he took note of their distress when he heard their cry."[15]

Jesus knew pain, and He knows ours.

He was betrayed, rejected and beaten. He literally sweat drops of blood, and He cried out to His Father.

I can see clearly now that healing came from "unanswered prayer," and hope was found when all felt lost. Little did I know, God was simmering salvation for my soul. He was breaking new ground to reveal a rotten root.

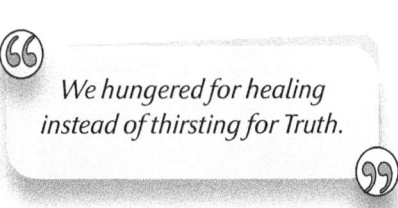
We hungered for healing instead of thirsting for Truth.

We hungered for healing instead of thirsting for Truth.

---

[14] 1 Peter 5:7
[15] Psalm 106:44

What I Couldn't See Before

Living with a chronic, incurable illness, an enduring, empty womb, a mangled marriage or a long-suffering season of singleness tests your theology, and suffering becomes your seminary.

Is this my fault? Is my faith too frail? Did I doubt the Divine? Or, is this a sacred calling for His glory? Was my pain a privilege? I had wrestled with "why", which opened a door to deception. Catch this, David (the man after God's own heart) asked "why." "My God, my God, why have you forsaken me? Why are you so far from saving me, so far from my cries of anguish? My God, I cry out by day, but you do not answer, by night, but I find no rest."[16]

And even Jesus questioned God in the throes of His suffering. Jesus felt abandoned and forsaken by His Father. Some of His last words came in questioning God!

"Eli, Eli, lema sabachthani?" Which means, My God, my God, why have you abandoned me?[17]

There's Hope to grab in His humanity. If the Savior of the world questioned and doubted, it is ok when we do.

Now, with the utmost of confidence, I can say that God was sweet to *Not* answer my prayer how I saw fit that dark December. Had I been rescued from physical pain; my soul would've continued to suffer. He didn't dismiss my distress. He set the scene for my spirit to be sifted, and that sift became salve for my soul. While physical pain still lingered, it brought permanent progress. I was free, free from bondage. The dirty devil's secret had been exposed, and I would learn to walk in the Truth of who Jesus says I am.

---

[16] Psalms 22:1-2
[17] Matthew 27:46

Remember Jacob and his wrestle with God?[18] After the wrestle, God gave him a new name, Israel. In my wrestle, <u>I didn't even know I needed a new name.</u>

Now I answer to: loved, worthy, forgiven, not because of what I have done, but because of what Jesus did.

And God, He is so worthy to be trusted.

When God mends our mind, He heals our hearts.

"For he has not despised or scorned the suffering of the afflicted one; he has not hidden his face from him but has listened to his cry for help."[19]

Joy Comes from the Mourning.

Grateful that my heart had been healed, I was still left with physical pain. We now felt released to seek a solution. My heart was at peace. My heart was ready. It was time to accept the inevitable and take another step towards healing.

But, first, I must take you back to where the root was planted, in high school. Sometimes, we have to go back before we can move forward.

---

[18] Genesis 32:22-32
[19] Psalms 22:24

CHAPTER TWO REFLECTIONS

1. "When he (Satan) lies, he speaks his native language, for he is a liar and the father of lies." John 8:44

   Ask God and those you trust what lies or negative beliefs you've been holding onto that need to be exposed. Jot them down.

   _____
   _____
   _____
   _____

2. "The Lord is near to the brokenhearted and saves those who are crushed in spirit." Psalm 34:18

   The Truth is that God never leaves you in your brokenness. He grieves with you.

   How can you become more aware of God's presence during difficult times?

   _____
   _____
   _____
   _____

3. "Submit yourselves, then, to God. Resist the devil, and he will flee from you." James 4:7

   Now that you've listed your lies from the enemy, how can you replace them with the Truth of God's Word?

   _____
   _____
   _____
   _____

4. "Therefore encourage one another and build each other up, just as in fact you are doing." 1 Thessalonians 5:11

   How can you support others who are also battling negative beliefs while dealing with their own distressing circumstances?

   _____
   _____
   _____
   _____

Chapter Three

Don't Sleep with Shame

The devil was devious one dark night.

As I woke up on an old, dingy couch, I sat up to my three friends staring, smirking across at me, from their own, dingy couch. They knew something I didn't, and I was the source of their smirk. What they proceeded to tell me would ultimately change the course of my life. The night before, we celebrated my best friend's birthday, irresponsibly and intoxicated. My poor choices left me powerless to defend myself.

I had been sexually assaulted.

My friends laughed as I learned of how it unfolded. I vaguely recall trying to defend myself. An unwanted and uninvited guest to the celebration was the culprit.

I gathered my things as I tripped on the truth of this trauma. I made my way home, hoping to avoid any interaction with my parents. Stunned, shocked and shamed, I had no words. Yes, I felt all those things because of what happened to me but more-so that my "friends" were in the room when it happened, did nothing to help and thought the whole thing was funny. What had happened?! Trauma took a toll, and it would take time to patch this pang.

The next twenty-four hours were a blur. I felt so dirty! I showered in shame. This shame would stick with me for quite some time. The enemy kept hissing that this was all my fault, that I deserved it. Yet, God just kept whispering, "Come home."

As a senior in high school, life had been carefree until now. (As I searched for a synonym for carefree, "devil-may-care" popped up as a similar word. Hmmm, isn't that interesting?!) I'm awestruck even by this revelation. The devil cared alright. He had cleverly crafted.

I was so asleep to my soul that I had mistaken destruction for satisfaction. My freewill had been in full gear.

I was raised in a warm, Christian home, and I remember praying the sinner's prayer when I was eight-years-old. My prayer was motivated by the abrupt passing of my grandmother. She was here one afternoon and gone that night. I feared death. This fear would haunt me longer than I care to admit. After a meeting with our pastor and praying for eternal assurance, I continued to wrestle with her loss. I was grateful for the peace of Heaven one day, but I had no idea we could live under an open heaven today. I did not know what it meant to have a relationship with Jesus. He certainly wasn't my Lord. I was having too much fun for Him to call the shots, until I wasn't.

As a kid, I lived for basketball. I had the privilege to travel and play the sport I loved. That came at a cost though. Yes, the financial cost my parents paid but also the constant sweeping away from church that found me disconnected from God and community that

I didn't know I needed. I loved basketball with everything I had, but it didn't love me back. As a freshman in high school, I suffered a torn ACL along with three other torn ligaments that made the tears more than trickle. Go big or go home, right?! I was a basketball player. That's all I knew.

That's what I did. That's who I was. That's where I belonged...in a gym. So, I floundered as a freshman and basketball friends faded. My loss of identity produced a prodigal. I began to pursue all the things of the world in search of something to soothe my soul. And I did, or so I thought.

We all tend to chase comfort at times, right? That relationship is risky, but it'll rescue me. Surely, that substance will substitute my sorrows. Parties - pure pleasure. We numb on Netflix and scroll through others' stories, so we don't have to tune into our own.

I have so much compassion for those that look to the world to mend their misery.

Speaking of misery, that was me. I was shamefully sorry for the life I had been living. One short-sighted decision isn't what launched me into trouble. This was a few years in the making. When I could no longer play the sport I loved, I didn't recognize who I was. So, the enemy began to rub his hands together, scheming "Now, it's game-time!"

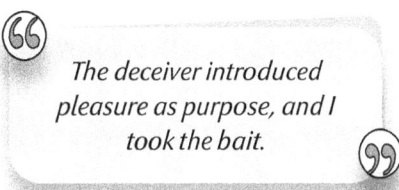

The deceiver introduced pleasure as purpose, and I took the bait.

He began to murmur lies just like he did to Eve in the garden. The deceiver introduced pleasure as purpose, and I took the bait.

I devoured the road to destruction. This season was full of sorrow for my mom and dad. They were parenting a prodigal. I owned it: rebellious, avoidant, arrogant, disrespectful, defiant and oblivious to the anguish I was causing. From boys to beverages to substances, I made one poor choice after the other. I had a hole in my soul, and I was trying to fill it. I chose to plug my pain with the vacuum of the world. The further I followed the world, following Jesus felt foreign.

Mom and Dad tried to get me back in church, but I was passive aggressive in my refusal. Sundays were sacred for them and secular for me, as I snoozed. Let's just say our meal wasn't the only thing we were cutting at Sunday lunch, the tension was indubitably thick. Our fractured relationship was of my own volition. My parents' attempts to make a U turn with my life left them throwing their hands up in exhaustion. They finally told me they feared I'd have to suffer natural consequences for refusing to listen any other way. I don't fault them for that at all.

At times, agony is the only adviser that will get our attention.

Which brings us to that dreadful night, my senior year. The consequences of my choices left me questioning everything. All along, I had claimed Jesus as my Savior. Not boldly and outwardly, but if asked. I felt like such a fraud. For all intense purposes, I was. The beauty in that brokenness is that, in His mercy, He still was and is my Savior. I did not know what it meant for Him to be Lord of my life, and clearly, my choices reflected such.

That repulsive night was a game-changer and an eye-opener. Satan intended to sabotage me, and sadly, he would for many years.

But God. He doesn't override our freewill. He Did Not cause this. He Did Not want this to happen. However, I truly believe He let my free will play out in this for my good, to wake me up to my self-destruction. Undoubtedly, my waywardness grieved His heart as it did my parents.

I'm a parent to teens myself now, and I ache when they make matters harder than they have to be. At times, they don't believe we know best.

But, I remember My journey and I trust God with their story!

"Train up a child in the way he should go, and when he is old, he will not depart from it."[20] The enemy meant to harm me that dreadful night. Instead, God's grace found me. Yes, grace.

"And we know that in all things God works for the good of those who love Him, who have been called according to His purpose."[21]

For the first time, I was painfully sobered by my sin and the damage I was doing. I was shocked by all He had spared me from.

God was working, and I was willing.

I was alone, ashamed, and I felt I could tell no one what had happened. In fact, I didn't tell a soul except for my boyfriend at the time. His attempt to "take care of" the perpetrator only caused more chaos and my trauma thickened. I did not talk to my parents about any of it. I concealed it in shame and my soul suffered for it.

That burden felt like a boulder, and I couldn't carry it any further.

So, one night, in the solitude of my room, I surrendered. I fell to my knees, and I wept, alone, with God. I profusely confessed my rebellion and fear of my future without Him. It was an "Ebenezer" moment to remember, repent and to profess to Jesus, "I'm yours. Whatever You want, I'll do it."

---

[20] Proverbs 22:6
[21] Romans 8:28

Little did I know the experience He was equipping me to encounter. He became Lord of my life that night.

The next two years proved to be a time of much needed rebuilding with my parents. The chapter to high school had closed, and I started to steer back on course. I chose to attend a local junior college and live at home. I continued to dabble in depravity though. It was hard to separate myself from the only "friends" I had known. I was well aware that we were headed different directions, and that honestly grieved me. I cared for these people. It was painful to pull away.

No, they weren't concerned for my best interest. Clearly, we'd established that. I was beginning to recognize that I was in bondage. Their company was comfort and simultaneously scary. I had nothing else to fall back on.

We're enslaved when we wear our bondage like a blanket.

We cozy up and convince ourselves that change is too complicated. To transition into new territory is no doubt terrifying. Challenging? Yes! But friend, it doesn't have to be complicated.

Fortunately, Jesus doesn't ask us to take giant leaps but small steps. So, little by little, I began to step out in faith to follow Him. "For we walk by faith, not by sight." 2 Corinthians 5:7

> *We're enslaved when we wear our bondage like a blanket.*

Soon after, God began to redeem the time lost with my parents. Not only did they become my best friends for a stint, they became my only friends. I LOVED serving them, making their lives easier after all the hell I had caused. I truly enjoyed cleaning the house for my mom, mowing the lawn for my dad and just altogether being "eyes up" on how I could help them. That was God, y'all. I was eighteen! Our Friday nights were special nights as we enjoyed dinner and a movie out. That time was a gift. The foundation of family was being fortified. God's goodness and my parents' prayers rallied me back into church. I confess that it was quite uncomfortable, at first.

The back row was where I sat solo as I tiptoed back to God.

The Holy Spirit then prompted me to tithe, and that was a leap of faith that landed me under the unlimited protection of our Father. I submitted my petite offering unbeknownst to the copious calling He had in store. God was preparing and priming me for what was next.

Friend, have you found yourself in a shady situation? Are your circumstances comfortable but not God's best? Are you, too, slumbering in shame? Imagine for a moment that we are sitting together on my now comfy, grace-filled couch. I am looking you in the eye. Yes, eyes up. I see you. You are immensely loved. Jesus offers you forgiveness and He wants to script a new soundtrack for your life. God is good to you. Today is your day! You can do hard things. You can walk away from the only way you've ever known. Everything is possible for the one who believes. You say, "But I don't believe I can change." Friend, I'll believe on your behalf. God believes in you. And it's not you that manufactures the modification, it's the Holy Spirit's work to do (John 15:26.) Allow me to pick up your mat of misery and lower it at His feet and say that the shackles aren't coming off someday but today. Don't let destruction destroy you. It's not too late. Don't postpone God's plans for you any longer.

What I Couldn't See Before

The Bible states that "If you declare with your mouth, "Jesus is Lord," and believe in your heart that God raised him from the dead, you will be saved. For it is with your heart that you believe and are justified, and it is with your mouth that you profess your faith and are saved. As Scripture says, "Anyone who believes in him will never be put to shame." For, "Everyone who calls on the name of the Lord will be saved."[22]

Friend, that's Good News!

You no longer have to sleep with shame.

This isn't about what we must do for God, but what He's already done for us. "For it is by grace you have been saved, through faith- and this is not from yourselves, it is the gift of God-not by works, so that no one can boast."[23]

If you've never confessed these words to our Creator, can I hold your hand while you do? Take a moment. Or find a friend to help you. Remember, it's not complicated.

Now, we are no longer slaves to our sin but slaves to righteousness. "You have been set free from sin and have become slaves to righteousness. Just as you used to offer yourselves as slaves to impurity and to ever-increasing wickedness, so now offer yourselves as slaves to righteousness leading to holiness."[24]

And, we all say "Amen!"

God doesn't just offer forgiveness of our sins, but He graciously gives us a new identity. When we receive His grace, we become Beloved sons and daughters. We're no longer defined by what we've done. Once Beloved, we get to experience His presence and walk in

---

[22] Romans 10:9-11, 13
[23] Ephesians 2:8-9
[24] Romans 6:18, 19

relationship with Him as we go about our days. And next, He places purpose on our lives as we partner with Him moving forward. How does one more forward, you say? One next step at a time. God speaks in sentences, not paragraphs. He invites us to follow as He leads. And remember, we now have a Companion in the Holy Spirit who will guide us as we go. I know, closing one chapter to start afresh may feel messy but it will be beautiful. "It (grace) teaches us to say "No" to ungodliness and worldly passions, and to live self-controlled, upright and godly lives in this present age."[25]

God has incredible purpose for your life that exceeds your wildest dreams and imagination.

As we wrap up, let me rewind. God was forecasting my future, and He's doing the same for you. He was on the precipice of calling me to something that required a slew of faith, packed with substantial surrender. As we turn the page to peek into my unknown, I'm cheering you on as you step into yours. I can attest that He was in my yesterday, so we can trust Him with tomorrow.

Let's do this thing - together!

---

[25] Titus 2:12

CHAPTER THREE REFLECTIONS

1. "If we confess our sins, He is faithful and just and will forgive us our sins and purify us from all unrighteousness." 1 John 1:9
   What moment in your life has brought you to the end of yourself and in need of confessing your wayward ways?
   Receive His forgiveness for you today.

   _____
   _____
   _____
   _____

2. "The Lord is compassionate and gracious, slow to anger, abounding in love. He will not always accuse, nor will he harbor his anger forever; he does not treat us as our sins deserve or repay us according to our iniquities." Psalm 103:8-10
   What area of your life do you need to revisit, sit with your younger self and show her/him compassion for what you went through?

   _____
   _____
   _____
   _____

3. "Therefore, if anyone is in Christ, the new creation has come: The old has gone, the new is here!" 2 Corinthians 5:17
    What steps can you take to rebuild your identity in Christ after a period of being lost, lonely and broken?

    _____
    _____
    _____
    _____

4. "And we know that in all things God works for the good of those who love him, who have been called according to his purpose." Romans 8:28
    What circumstances in your life have either happened to you, or you have done, that you need to entrust to God, knowing He'll work it for your good?

    _____
    _____
    _____
    _____

Chapter Four

Courage Over Comfort

The only light in my room was my computer screen as I knocked out an assignment for school. Now, it took a minute because this was in the "dial-up" days. To my Gen Z peeps and younger, dial-up is what you did to gain access to the internet through your telephone network. Smart phones weren't in existence yet. No, I didn't just open my Mac and go. It was a process. And yes, antiquated. I feel antiquated in this moment. But, let me remind you, I fall just on the cusp of being a millennial. Now that we've discussed that archaic access and my neighboring relevance to the cool kids, let's move on.

As I listened and waited to the screeching, squawking sound while dial up connected, the Holy Spirit began to dial in. My time in junior college was in its last semester. What was next? I had applied to the local university in my hometown and been accepted. This felt like an obvious next step to follow junior college. But God began to speak. University of North Texas (UNT) and University of Texas - Tyler (UT Tyler) came out of nowhere as options to consider. Huh? I'd literally never even heard of these places. Denton, Texas? Where on earth is that? God prompted me to pursue them anyways. So, eons later (remember the delay of dial-up,) I did a deep-dive and researched both schools.

God was showing me that I had become too comfortable in my circumstances. This season and time had been for the purpose of reconciling with my parents. God had been so very kind to mend our relationship. I was grateful. He also had illuminated that I was beginning to rely on them more than Him.

There comes a time when comfort curbs cultivation.

When a mama eagle is priming her chicks to fly, she gradually removes items from the nest that make it comfy. The nest starts to poke and prod a bit. The mama realizes this must be done, or they'll never leave the nest. They wouldn't have a reason to. Furry feathers from their bed begin to fall, rounded rations reduced, all to prep her precious fledglings to fly. She knows they weren't born merely to reside in the refuge of a burrow. They were meant to mount up and SOAR!

Friend, discomfort drives development. Did you know you were meant to soar? "But those who hope in the Lord will renew their strength. They will soar on wings like eagles; they will run and not grow weary; they will walk and not be faint."[26] When we feel the poke and prod of the Holy Spirit, be encouraged. An invitation to

---

[26] Isaiah 40:31

more freedom is on its way. Can you imagine anything more freeing than an eagle in its element?

The climb to freedom is unquestionably uncomfortable, but remember that for which you were created for, to soar over your circumstances, not succumb to them.

I remember going into my parent's room that night and telling them what transpired. You could tell that they wanted to believe this was God, but the hesitation in their hearts was undeniable… and understandable. I'm sure their thoughts went something like this, "God, we just got her back. Now, we're supposed to let her go?!" Or "God, are you sure she's ready for this?",

"Has she been dialed in with you long enough to not get distracted and deterred by the world again?" Here's what they actually said, "Honey, if this is something you feel you're being called to, then let's talk it over, tomorrow. It's late." I'd imagine their prayer was, "Oh Lord! We believe. Help us with our unbelief." Remember, rebellion had been my recent routine.

The next day turned into next month, and we made a weekend of it. We traveled and toured both campuses. Mind you, UNT was having their annual Arts and Jazz Festival that weekend, and let's just say it was a colorful crowd. Art was being expressed in outward, bold fashion. This was a culture shock. My conservative, southern Baptist parents were wide-eyed with eyebrows raised. I admit that I was a tad taken aback, as well. Art was not yet conveyed and displayed in our west Texas town like that. My parents proceeded with caution. "Honey, are you sure this seems like a good idea?"

What I Couldn't See Before

Adventure was calling, and I was like "Yea, I think maybe so." You could see it again, "Oh Lord! We believe. Help us with our unbelief." UT Tyler was beautiful, calm, quiet, and surely a safer spot to secure my next step.

Buuuuuut, oftentimes, God doesn't call us to safe, does He?

So, you guessed it, UNT in Denton, Texas, was calling my name. Or, better yet, God was inviting me to step out in radical obedience to follow Him into the unknown. This was a total leap of faith. I did not know a single soul in that town nor anyone, anywhere near it. Over the next few months, we made a handful of trips back and forth in order to find a job, an apartment and to gain a general idea of the area. We also looked into church options. I knew that church would be my connection to community, and it was imperative that I connect. Otherwise, I knew my propensity to long for belonging among misguided masses. We landed at a local, Bible-believing church that had a considerable college crowd.

School: Check
Apartment: Check
Job: Check
Church: Check

My focus evolved into preparing for farewell. My heart had three roommates: anticipation, fear and grief. I was crazy excited for my future regardless of the unknown. I was also afraid to leave all I had known. I had come to savor weekly lunches with both sets of grandparents. They spoiled me with scrambled egg sandwiches. They loved me lavishly and intentionally in preparing for our gathering each time. Coffee, creamer and conversation was our sweet spot. The familiar faces of family would fade in consistency, and that broke me. I was holding hands with goodbye and hello. To ease the exit, we decided it best for me to find a 4-legged friend. We perused the paper (Yes, a black and white newspaper people,

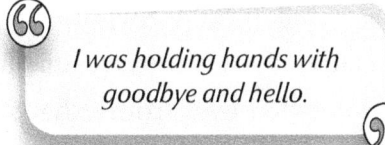
I was holding hands with goodbye and hello.

the one you held in your hand, the one you circled things on and picked up your landline to call & inquire about things from.) Nope, online social outlets didn't exist at that time to search for canine companions. After multiple calls, we drove out to the country and claimed my pup, my Jack Russell Terrier that we named Max. Max would be my saving grace many, many times while navigating the choppy waters of change. I remember one night in particular that my mom and I were walking Max. I told her I knew that this was going to be the hardest thing I had ever done, but I just knew I had to do it. Max and I were ready to conquer the world.

On a steamy summer day, we departed West Texas and started out towards Denton. This was a solid 5 ½ hour distance from home. Side note, no, we did not have GPS. Gosh, the more I write, the more dated I feel. I'll also note that we had a trailer loaded down with my hard-earned Goodwill purchases to furnish my humble abode. I also found a couch from the newspaper ads. Our caravan looked like a scene from the Beverly Hillbillies, an old show that starred a country bumpkin family that had all their belongings placed in such disarray in their wagon. To prove my point, we had to pullover en route because one of the boxes flew out of the trailer and my possessions were plastered on the pavement. Funny, not funny.

Eventually, we made our way into D town. We knew the heat back home but not humidity. The stickiness was a slap in the face and sweat soaked my poor dad. Unloading began. Piece by piece, we curated a cushy space for Max and me. That night, we laid in my loft, bowled over from exhaustion and slumber came swiftly. The next day dawned, pics were hung in place, fridge was full and now our hearts would be momentarily emptied. Goodbye was upon us, and I was in a crevice of learning how very near God was when my family was so far. The dreadful words were spoken but not without scheduling my first trip back home. We needed something to look forward to, to soften the sayonara. And then, there came the time to let them go and them leave me to grow. Oh, the heaviness I felt that day. Max and I made it through our first night together, and we managed to mosey downstairs the next morning to mix up some breakfast. It was a new day and a new dawn.

I had never followed God that audaciously. I did not know what my future held, but I knew Who held my future. This was a total trust fall. Jesus, I don't know why you called me to Denton, but because you said so, I am here. There's a story in Genesis where Abram, later named Abraham, was on his way to Canaan with his family. (Abraham was known for being the father of many nations. God promised him that he would have more descendants than there were stars in the sky, including us.) Abram's father, Terah, was leading the pack. Then, something devastating happened. "...But when they came to Harran, they settled there."[27]

It goes on to say that Abraham's father died in Harran. How very sad! Complacency blocked God's best for Terah.

---

[27] Genesis 11:31

Let's keep reading. Just one chapter later, "The Lord said to Abram, "Go from your country, your people and your father's household to the land I will show you."[28]

God promised Abram abundance. "So Abram went, as the Lord had told him."[29]

I did not want to settle. I wanted faith like Abram. I desired courage over comfort. Friend, when we leap out in life with Jesus, He will not let us fall.

Friends, where are your circumstances complacent? Do you worship the idol of ease? Is He inviting you to lay down your life of leisure and join Him for an adventure? Can I appeal to you that He is worth it Every. Single. Time! Don't buy the lie that the Christian life is drab and boring. Don't settle for mediocre Christianity. Go all in with Jesus and watch what He will do. Will it be easy? Most assuredly, no. "In this world you will have trouble. But take heart! I have overcome the world." John 16:33b Will it be rewarding? Heck yeah! "A thief comes only to steal and kill and destroy. I have come so that they may have life and have it in abundance."[30] Don't allow the thief to take anymore. Chase abundance!

---

[28] Genesis 12:1
[29] Genesis 12:4
[30] John 10:10

What I Couldn't See Before

My new zip code was scary, no doubt. It was also a place of utter dependence on Jesus, and that's not a bad place to be. Trying, yes, but an opportunity to be stretched and molded beyond my comfort. Step by step, I set off to work. I trekked to school. Max and I explored the local parks. I plunged myself into the local church, knowing I needed to plug in with like-minded people. I joined a girls' Bible study, and I sought out a mentor. I was doing all I could to acclimate. I met people here and there, but I was struggling to make a solid connection. That was God. He wasn't ready for me to add anyone to the equation of He and I. He had me to Himself, and I'm confident that's what He wanted for the time being. I was learning to live on my own, and that built my confidence. I was growing in relationship with my mentor, and they would occasionally have me over for dinner. Max (my jovial Jack Russell) was a Godsend, and I felt seen in his salutations. His unconditional love and excitement sustained me. Routinely, when I was away, he'd work his way upstairs and then down with one of my red house shoes. When I arrived home, I'd find him in the recliner, snuggling with said shoe. Unfortunately, my solitary situation made me weary. I longingly ached for family and the comfort of home. In fact, I went home as often as I could. I was so motivated to graduate so I could move back. I even told my grandpa one night, while enjoying supper, that I'd be departing Denton the moment diploma was in hand. He looked me straight in the eye, with a slow shake of his head and said, "Sugar, you won't ever move back. You're going to meet Mr. Twinkle, and that'll be it." At the time, that did not sound dreamy in the least. I naively told him, "No way, Pa. I'm coming home." I remember crying every time I left family for my lonely loft. Now, that may sound pathetic or desperate to some, but it was painful and I was desperate. I recall one night at my girls' Bible study. At the end, when prayer requests were collected, my containment collapsed. I shared my cry for community and how very lost in loneliness I was. I even said that I'd love to be invited for coffee or something. No One Called Me. Not even the leader. Now, while the enemy meant that to harm me, I chose to trust that God intended that for my good. Again, God was establishing His rightful place and I wasn't ready for the added assurances.

We're not meant to plug the pain of our soul with temporary fillers. Instead, we pause with God until He pulls through on His promises.

I found myself calling my parents at midday, in between classes. With apprehension, they'd ask how I was doing, and that opened the floodgates. I was just so terribly lonely. Finally, they'd endured all they could. My dad told me that I could come home that day if I wanted to. I cannot imagine how helpless they felt with my relentless return to tears. I didn't know why, but I told them I couldn't go home. Something within me knew I had to stick it out even though I was tempted to tuck and run. This lasted a long 9 months or more.

But then, the breakthrough broke through. I learned to find solace in solitude. Jesus became my Jam. Max and I jogged with joy. Friendships emerged, and I began to run in my lane. God had secured his position as priority in my life, and then He began to place people in my path.

Soon after, I was prepping to lead a young group of college girls at my church. I knew what it felt like to be in unfamiliar territory, and I desired to give them a safe place to belong. The church required you to go through intensive training before leading. I was excited to jump in, and that's where the enemy crept in. The formula for leading felt like I didn't fit the mold. My resume wasn't spotless. The tactic used for living "above reproach" was fear. I really battled the bombarding thoughts the tempter threw my way. "Who are you to lead these girls?!" "You're not qualified." "Remember what you've done?!" I'm grateful I had the sage advice from my mentor to see me through it. I realize now what was happening…religion wasn't relinquishing. Sin management was the destination, and Jesus wasn't our compass. Sadly, shame was a strategy the ministry used to keep us in line. I mean, I get it…you're talking about college students here that you're equipping to lead. Guardrails were needed, for sure. But, holding your repentant, former sin against you, not cool and not God's tactic.

The Bible shares countless cases of faulty yet faithful people that God used to advance His Kingdom. Adam, and Eve (come on now, they both played a part) broke a boundary and then they hid in shame. That fateful fruit. All of humanity still advanced though. Abraham and Sarah were impatient and took matters into their own hands. I mean, who could blame them?! Abraham was already seventy-five when God first shared His promise of children to come. To say they were no spring chickens is quite an understatement, don't you think? Fast forward 10 years or so, they felt the need to help God fulfill His promise to them (We're all guilty of thinking God needs our help, right?) of having more descendants than they could count. So, they agreed to have Abraham sleep with the maidservant, Hagar to conceive. God did not extend His blessing through that child. He fulfilled His promise through both Abraham and Sarah by blessing them with Isaac. Abraham was 100-years-old when this Finally came to fruition. And God still granted Abraham endless ancestors even though he and Sarah didn't trust Him at times and took matters into their own hands, or tents. Noah heard from God, obeyed, built the ark by faith, no rain in sight with I'm sure plenty of mockers along the way, but then he was the first to get drunk in the Bible, and his sons had to cover his naked body. And yet, we have the rainbow, and the promise it holds, as a result of Noah's obedience. Moses more than lost his temper at the unjust treatment of the slaves, (his people) and killed a man then ran in shame. And yet, God called and positioned Moses to lead the Israelites to freedom. Through God, Moses managed the miracle of a parted sea and they walked on dry ground to ultimately experience an ocean of emancipation.

David let his eyes lead to lust, then he slept with another man's wife. Next, he purposely placed her husband on the front lines in battle for him to die. And God Still said David was a man after God's own heart. Rahab was a prostitute, but she helped hide the Israelites and then aided in their escape when they were scoping out the promised land. King Solomon, he strayed and worshipped idols. He ended up with more wives than I'm even comfortable typing, and they led to his destruction. They pulled him away from God. But, he was still known as the wisest man, You guys, don't miss it, Jesus descended from this lineage. That was His family tree. Can you believe it?!

Paul, formerly Saul used to orchestrate not just persecution of Christians but the execution of them, too. Then, God blinded Saul for 3 days to get his attention. He had a revolutionary transformation, God gave him a new name, and then he became a legendary leader

What I Couldn't See Before

for the Gospel. Martha, man, she was worried and upset about a lot, right? She was so focused and fixated on doing that she missed being with Jesus. And Peter, we can't forget about Peter. Poor Peter. He had had such great intentions, but his vision was skewed. He never saw himself denying Jesus, but he did... three. different. times. The woman at the well had a serious commitment crisis. She had not one, not two, but five different husbands and was living with another man and yet she couldn't contain her excitement after connecting with Jesus. She shared her encounter with the entire community.

AND GOD USED THEM ALL!

Whew! Do you feel like you can stand a little taller and walk a little lighter now? Me too, friend. Me too. Shame is often a strategy used to silence and stall. We read it above, and we experience it ourselves. But mistakes are what make us human...and humble. Perfection is not the prize.

God uses the broken not the blameless to reveal the beauty of His redemption.

Can you imagine if the stories Scripture shares were spotless?! That would feel unattainable. I'm so grateful the Bible is relatable and relevant even today. The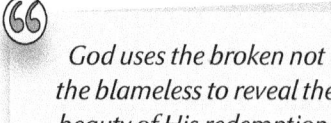

> *God uses the broken not the blameless to reveal the beauty of His redemption.*

stories within It all point us to Jesus. That's what we get to do and what I did. I leaned in, confessed that I could not lead without Him and continued to encourage those sweet, young women. I told shame where to go, and I went on my way. That was a festive season for my faith.

I continued to meet with my mentor. She was a prudent place to perch while I traipsed through the doubt. She even helped me to dream about my future. I imagined myself as a single gal with my work purse, traveling to and from work. She began to help me consider the prospect of marriage. Did I even desire that or was I denying myself that desire because I did not feel I deserved it? Was my lack of entertaining the idea that of self-protection? Why yes, yes it was. I feared when someone learned of my past, they'd no longer yearn for a future with me. My mentor told me that when I met the right guy, they wouldn't care where I'd been but only where I was going.

That goes for all of us, with Jesus. Jesus doesn't hold our past against us. He doesn't remind us of our mistakes. He invites us to follow Him, to trust again, and He promises a future, "For I know the plans I have for you," declares the Lord, "plans to prosper you and not to harm you, plans to give you hope and a future."[31]

God had a promising prospect on the horizon for me, and He holds a favorable future for you.

---

[31] Jeremiah 29:11

CHAPTER FOUR REFLECTIONS

1. "The Lord had said to Abram, 'Go from your country, your people and your father's household to the land I will show you.'" Genesis 12:1

   How can you respond to God's call to step out of your comfort zone and trust Him with your future?

   _____
   _____
   _____
   _____

2. "Do not love the world or anything in the world. If anyone loves the world, love for the Father is not in them." 1 John 2:15

   How can you recognize and overcome the idols of comfort and complacency in your life?

   _____
   _____
   _____
   _____

3. "The Lord is my strength and my shield; my heart trusts in him, and he helps me." Psalm 28:7

   In what ways is God inviting you to rely more on Him rather than on others?

   _____
   _____
   _____
   _____

4. "But grow in the grace and knowledge of our Lord and Savior Jesus Christ." 2 Peter 3:18

   How can you embrace the discomfort that comes with spiritual growth and transformation?

   _____
   _____
   _____
   _____

5. "And let us consider how we may spur one another on toward love and good deeds, not giving up meeting together, as some are in the habit of doing, but encouraging one another—and all the more as you see the Day approaching." Hebrews 10:24-25

   How can you find and cultivate a supportive faith community and build meaningful connections with other believers?

   _____
   _____
   _____
   _____

Chapter Five

Trust the Process

My mentor had me over for what seemed like a simple supper on a Sunday. Pot roast, gravy and we ladled ourselves in lengthy conversation. She began to probe me about meeting a potential someone. Unbeknownst to me, her and her best friend had been scheming for this someone and I to meet. This prospect had recently graduated from UNT, but he was still serving and connected in the college ministry at the church we all attended. His name was Robert, or better yet, Rob.

These two women joined forces, for a month or so, in an attempt to intersect our paths. We both expressed that we didn't want to be set up. So, we continued in our separate ways until a softball game popped up in conversation. Rob played recreational softball. He decided he'd meet me but wanted to keep it low key; hence, the game. He thought, if nothing else, he could try and connect me with some people since I was still relatively new to town. My mentor then proposed the idea to me. At first, I hem-hawed around and was like, "Umm, I don't know. Are you sure this is a good idea?" All the doubts doused me. Yet, I reluctantly agreed to go. What did I have to lose?

My sister was in town for a short stay when the decision had been made, so we thought it best for me to find something to wear. But it couldn't be too cute. Casual, seemingly careless, yet intentional, and fitting for the occasion. Don't try too hard, but put forth your best pitch. The summer night came, and I was up. Would I hit it out of the park? Or, was this all for nothing? I arrived at the ballpark with the two mentors and one of their sons that was twelve. We all watched the game, but I couldn't tell you a thing about it. All I remember was his smile. We met once the game was over, and we all thought it would be fun to hop in the suburban and drive on over to Sonic. I know, I know, romantic, eh? While we sipped on our slushies, chatting came easily...for him. You guys, this was so unfamiliar to me. To add to the awkwardness, the 12-year-old intrusively leaned into our chat from the backseat. We had an eager eyewitness to it all. The night ended with Rob asking for my number, and that he intended to invite me to some gatherings with his group.

Rob called me the next day, as promised, and suggested I join him with some friends for the night. He picked me up, as a gentleman should, and he introduced me to all his people. I was still out of sorts, you guys. I felt out of place, unknown and this was not the crowd I was used to.

Socials with substances, filled with shallow exchanges was my norm. These guys were kind, friendly, genuinely cared to know me and didn't need outside sources to extend their enjoyment.

This crowd loved Jesus!

My engagement was guarded, but my heart was hopeful.

Our next interaction was an infinitely long phone call that hung on for hours. As it turns out, we had several similarities. Both of our parents had been married before, but they had now been married for over twenty-five years. And we both shared a similar upbringing in church. These correlations brought connection. One on one dates were a Big "no no" in the ministry we were a part of, so he invited me on a double date with his roommate and his girlfriend. We had a really great time together. My soul was stirring, but I was uneasy. I feared this would fail once he knew my former ways. Well, wouldn't you know it, as he drove me home, he dove into the depths of discussion. He shared his Jesus story with me, and I started to sweat with trepidation. His journey with Jesus had seemed mostly flawless. Oh no! He was about to ask me my story. This was our third time together, and he was wasting no time. I was already thinking, "Well, this was fun while it lasted. It was great knowing you." I confess I didn't hear the tail-end of his tale because God was giving me a pep talk. Deep breath, Linsey. All you

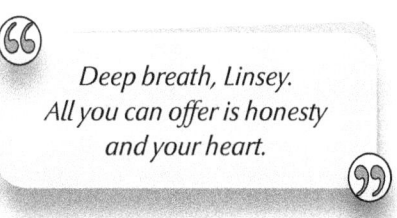

Deep breath, Linsey. All you can offer is honesty and your heart.

can offer is honesty and your heart. So, there I went. My tale was tainted. My past wasn't pretty. Shame slapped me again.

Remember, my mentor told me, "Linsey, when you meet the one, he won't care where you've been. He'll only care where you're going." My saga was shared, and then I just stared straight ahead as we rode. As we pulled into the parking lot, my palpitations paused until he responded. He put his 4-Runner in park. He turned towards me. He placed his hand on mine. And friend, these are the VERY words that came out of his mouth! As he locked eyes with mine (shame wanted mine to sink) he said, "I don't care where you've been. I only care where you're going." Seriously! I cannot make this up! I had no words. Shame expected departure, but grace grabbed me and wouldn't let me go. I didn't know what to do with myself. Rob didn't know the weight of his words. All I did was chew on his comment relentlessly, like gum that's nervously gnawed on until it loses its flavor.

Have you ever experienced the grace of God from an unexpected someone before? Their look, their words, are an undeniable representation of Jesus. You fear judgement, but you encounter acceptance instead? This makes me think of the story of the woman at the well in John 4. Jesus had made his way into a town called Sychar. It was high noon. Jesus was tired, so he stopped at a well. A Samaritan woman was making her way to the same well. Pause. At this time, Samaritans and Jews did not associate with one another. And, men certainly did not comingle with women. Furthermore, this woman was approaching the well at what would've been the hottest time of day. An inopportune time to draw water unless you had an unknown, divine appointment with the Living Water! This woman was forced to walk to this well at such an unfavorable time because she was shunned by society. She was not welcome with the other women when they went for water, in the cool of the morning. She had a history with men, many men and multiple marriages that never panned out. So, she walked alone but not without the accompaniment of her humiliation. She landed at the well, and Jesus was there to meet her.

"Jesus said to her, "Will you give me a drink?" This was a sacred, private moment with Jesus and this woman. Remember, no one else was there at this time of day. "The Samaritan woman said to him, "You are a Jew and I am a Samaritan woman. How can you ask me for a drink?" "Jesus answered her, "If you knew the gift of God and who it is that asks you for a drink, you would have asked him and he would have given you living water." "Sir," the woman said, "you have nothing to draw with and the well is deep. Where can you get this living water?" "Jesus answered, "Everyone who drinks this water will be thirsty again, but whoever drinks the water I give them will never thirst. Indeed, the water I give them will become in them a spring of water welling up to eternal life." The woman, in desperation for this living water He spoke of, asked Jesus to give it to her. Her soul had dried up from her sin. "Sir, give me this water so that I won't get thirsty and have to keep coming here to draw water." "He told her, "Go, call your husband and come back." "I have no husband," she replied." "Jesus said to her, "You are right when you say you have no husband. The fact is, you have had five husbands, and the man you now have is not your husband. What you have just said is quite true." A moment later, she tells Jesus, "I know that Messiah (called Christ) is coming. When he comes, he will explain everything to us." *Then Jesus declared, I, the one speaking to you — I am He.*[32]

Mic drop. Can you imagine?! Sweat is running down her back while tears stream down her face. Maybe there was the slightest, refreshing breeze as she realized she'd met with the Messiah. The heat was heavy, but her heart was lighter than it had been in a long

---

[32] John 4:4-26 paraphrased

time. I wonder if her jaw and water jar dropped in unison. One encounter with Jesus changed everything.

"Then, leaving her water jar, (Don't miss it! She left her water jar! She left her old way of living, of thinking, of believing and sin patterns. She experienced the Living Water, and her yearning was forever quenched.) the woman went back to the town and said to the people, "Come, see a man who told me everything I ever did. Could this be the Messiah?" "They came out of the town and made their way toward him."

And here is the most beautiful part: "Many of the Samaritans from that town believed in him BECAUSE OF THE WOMAN'S TESTIMONY, "He told me everything I ever did."[33]

God can redeem anything. He can restore the worst parts of us. He can use the ugliest chapters of our stories to reveal the beauty of His mercy and forgiveness. There's a saying, "Sin will take you further than you want to go, keep you longer than you want to stay and cost you more than you want to pay." This had been her mantra, and she was desperate for a new one. So, what if grace took us further than we ever imagined, left the door unlocked and kept an open tab.

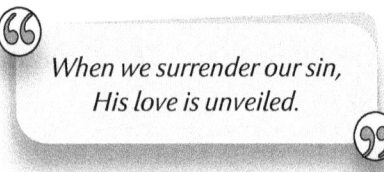
When we surrender our sin, His love is unveiled.

When we surrender our sin, His love is unveiled.

---

[33] John 4:39

This woman had come face to face with grace and so had I. I shared my unsightly story with Rob, he stayed, and I was undone. He would prove to be steady in showing me God's grace, and I would struggle to receive it. Our acquaintanceship fell to fast friendship, and he flew into meet my family Labor Day weekend. He was staggered by the size of our west Texas tumbleweeds, and my family was shocked I had landed such a gem. The guys I'd dated prior to Rob were…let's just say, not nuptially notable. The weekend was effortless, enjoyable and oh so natural. Furthermore, my grandpa confirmed that I had, indeed, met Mr. Twinkle. We were now quickly on our way to courtship.

Alas, my excruciating era of loneliness had finally petered out. That makes me wonder, have you ever been in a season that showed no signs of ceasing? Have you had nights relentlessly stretch into morning as slumber evaded you? Your constant breakdowns a beat down? You ask why?

Why is this so hard? Does this have an end? When will my poor pillow get a break since it's still soggy from last night's sobbing? God's word says, "You've kept track of my every toss and turn through the sleepless nights, each tear entered into your ledger, each ache written in your book."[34] Are some of you saying, "God, you're gonna need a bigger ledger?!" Friend, He can hold them all. My son's coach says to his players often, "Trust the process." Notice, he didn't say "Understand the process." I had to trust Him in the process.

---

[34] Psalms 56:8 (MSG)

Think of Noah. He undoubtedly had to trust the process. Surely people thought Noah was crazy for building an enormous boat with no rainfall in sight. And, I'd imagine he felt pretty alone in it all. But, he had the faith to trust the process. His faith was fueled before the flood, and he stayed steady before the wind and waves came. I can only imagine the deep satisfaction he felt, floating (figuratively and literally) those forty days, knowing he had patiently persisted in following God. That olive branch was a sign of new life and a fresh start. "The dove came back to him in the evening, and there, in her beak, was a fresh olive leaf. So, Noah knew that the water level had subsided from the earth."[35] Noah's journey was arduous but fruitful. And because of his obedience, he got to witness the faithfulness of God and experience His promises to be true. "Whenever the rainbow appears in the clouds, I will see it and remember the everlasting covenant between God and all living creatures of every kind on the earth."[36]

From trial to triumph, we're called to trust the process. Now and again, God reveals the reason for the rigorous road but oftentimes, He won't. That's where we must believe that He is working it all in our favor. He's always in our corner.

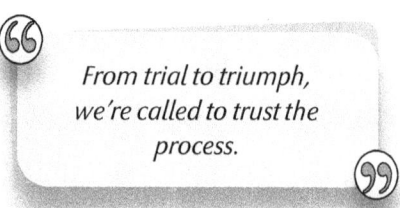

From trial to triumph, we're called to trust the process.

---

[35] Genesis 8:11
[36] Genesis 9:16

Without question, my lonely, one-on-one season with Jesus sealed my solidarity with Him. Jesus took His time to settle onto the throne of my heart before allowing other relationships to make their way into my life. Jesus had established that He was #1, and now I could enjoy God WITH Rob. Not the other way around. Order matters in the Kingdom. Otherwise, I'd have developed an unhealthy dependence on Rob to fulfill what only God can do.

It's worth noting that I told Rob if he didn't jive with my terrier, Max then none of it would work. Fortunately, they shared a fondness for one another. I'd also like to mention that I grew up hunting with my dad, another main man of mine. I had been walking, hand in hand, in the coal- black, before dawn with my dad since I was eight. It was imperative we settled in before the wildlife woke. His hand was all I needed to trust, that as my guide, he had me when I couldn't even see one step in front of us. On these trips, my dad and I had few words. It was glorious. It was quiet. It was peaceful. It was special. I sometimes even snagged a killer nap as we sat so still for hours in hopes that a deer would trek our way. One Fall morning, I struck luck with a buck. I wasn't so lucky in one way. The shot recoiled, and the scope did a number just between my eyes. It was attractive, let me tell ya. Now, my dad taught us that if we claim it, we clean it. So, I had to dress that deer out like the best of 'em. Later that day, Rob was planning to join us. It was time to make our way into town to meet him. I had a bruiser between my eyes and bloody bib overalls. I was a sight for somebody, that's for sure. We pulled into our local McDonald's, and my dad proceeded to tell me that I could go in all by myself to get Rob. He thought that was the funniest shenanigan, me walking in there looking like I did. I needed no help in being humbled. I waltzed in there to grab Rob.

He had quite the smirk on my arrival. Later that afternoon, we went back out for Rob to have his fair chance at securing some venison. While waiting, I asked my dad for the necessary papers in order to sneak off to go to the bathroom. Rob seemed quite surprised at my ease of going in the woods. After spending the afternoon outdoors, we drove back up to the house and enjoyed a sweltering pot of stew over an open campfire. That night, of All nights, Rob affirmed his love for me. I did not expect to hear those three words after my unalluring actions that day. But, what seemed to seal the deal for him were two things: 1. Seeing my interaction with my dad and 2. That a girl knew how to go in the woods.

To all my single ladies out there, now you know how to win one. You're welcome.

Before long, we began to dream of marriage. Rob was a football coach, and I was still in college. Football in Texas is almost it's own denomination. Sacrifices are made in light of that profession. The cost to coach is high, and time off is rare. So, we contemplated my line of work and what would work best around his calling. We knew time off together was priority and would be scarce if I chose the corporate route. You guys, we even penciled in wedding dates, and we weren't even engaged. But, the window to wed was tight when football had its thumb on us.

My parents stated a few years prior that if and when I ever desired marriage, college diploma must come first. This unwritten rule was of utmost importance to them. I didn't anticipate what came next. My parents rang me up one night, and they proceeded to tell me that we had their blessing if we wanted to marry before I graduated. Excuse me, what? This is what I heard, "Linsey, you've somehow landed a good one. Please don't screw this up." Now, I was the one saying, "Lord, I believe. Help me with my unbelief."

We were floored by their proposal, and that freed us up to start pursuing our future, together.

CHAPTER FIVE REFLECTIONS

1. "For I know the plans I have for you," declares the Lord, "plans to prosper you and not to harm you, plans to give you hope and a future." Jeremiah 29:11

    How can you trust that God's timing and provision in relationships is perfect, even when it requires patience and faith in the waiting and loneliness?

    _____
    _____
    _____
    _____

2. "So do not fear, for I am with you; do not be dismayed, for I am your God. I will strengthen you and help you; I will uphold you with my righteous right hand." Isaiah 41:10

    How can you trust God's call to step out in bold faith, even when it involves uncertainty and potential rejection?

    _____
    _____
    _____
    _____

3. "Let us then approach God's throne of grace with confidence, so that we may receive mercy and find grace to help us in our time of need." Hebrews 4:16

   How can you overcome the traps of shame and embrace God's grace and mercy in your life?

   _____
   _____
   _____
   _____

4. "Many of the Samaritans from that town believed in him because of the woman's testimony." John 4:39

   In what ways is God calling you to share your story to inspire and encourage others?

   _____
   _____
   _____
   _____

Chapter Six

Grappling with Grace

Friends, I really hope you're sitting for this chapter. It's a doozie! Football season came and went. Rob's time of haste and hustle was winding down. Christmas was upon us, and I was excited to be home for the break. Per usual, I would help my dad each year in shopping for my mom. He often found himself in a tizzy over what to get her. So, each December, I did my due diligence in helping him nail down the ideal gift. As we pulled into the mall, I hit my dad up that we should get a bottle of wine to celebrate the holiday. You know, add to the jubilee. Now, this wasn't a regular request I made, but I was feeling spontaneous and light-hearted. My dad looked at me as he turned the corner and said, "With Rob's parents coming?!" (Rob's parents didn't partake in spirited beverages.) I then replied with, "Rob's parents are coming?!" We locked eyes, and he said "Oh, #*&@!" I immediately burst out laughing. It was hilarious and cute. He stared so somberly and was like, "Don't say a word!" Our lips sealed tight with the news of their arrival. We purchased my mom's present, and we left the wine at the store. Then, onto home we went.

Don't worry. Rob found out a few years later about Dad spilling the secret of their surprise stay.

The intent of Rob's family coming was greater than I thought. Rob was planning to propose to me with all our loved ones present. However, there was one slight hiccup. He didn't have the ring. He had custom made a beauty, but he was advised that if he shipped it out of state and back, then he wouldn't have to pay taxes on it. So, he proceeded, and he found himself empty handed. Our time together as families was pleasant, but incredibly awkward with the elephant consuming the room. His parents left, and he hadn't popped the question. He stayed behind to head back when I did. He and my dad went to lunch, and my dad just straight up asked him what he was waiting on. Rob shared his embarrassment that he had no ring. My dad told him I wouldn't care (I didn't,) and to just ask me. So, that night, at halftime of a Bowl game, Rob got down on one knee in their front yard, and he asked me to marry him. I didn't need a ring to say yes. Rob saw in me what I didn't yet see in myself, and I knew God was gifting me with a man that was a tangible representation of His love for me.

Texas won the Bowl game that year, and Rob won my heart. We made our way back to Denton, and we hit the ground running with plans. Initially, we had booked the church we both called home. My dream was to get married on a beach, barefoot though. But our budget didn't lend to a coastal covenant, so we settled for the fellowship hall. Both of our mentors were invited into the planning process. One day, while at work, my mentor rang me up. She asked, "So, for the reception, would you rather have plain table skirts or pleated ones?" I'm sorry. I had to filter my words because I was grateful for her help, but I honestly didn't care. Why did that detail even matter? I'm not a girl that had dreamed up every ounce of detail pertaining to my big day. I completely respect and support those that do. That just wasn't me. I really just desired a beach, elegant bridal portraits, and I didn't have strong opinions about anything else. I had prayed for a spiritual leader, and the Lord had provided. The rest was inessential to me.

Rob began to research honeymoon options, and he happened upon a "wedding-moon" package. Basically, if you booked so many nights at this resort, they provided your wedding at no additional cost, and that included everything. Rob thought he had struck gold. He called me with such excitement only to be utterly confused by my response. I was like, "Well, we've already invested in the planning here and all those details. Do we want to change all of that now?!" Linsey, what is your problem?! Fellas, if you're reading this, I want to apologize on behalf of females for confusing the heck out of you sometimes. There are moments when we don't even know what we want. To make matters worse, as a 1 on the enneagram, I struggle with change or spontaneity. So, even though this sounded amazing, my initial response was one of hesitation. I needed time to change course. But, it didn't take long for me to throw those table skirts to the wind and envision those bare feet on the sand. Our families were on board, and we all booked our stay. Mind you, Rob and I would not be staying together before our big day. My maid of honor and I would share a room at the couples' resort where Rob and I would be, and Rob would stay with his best man and our family at another resort. We had to get clearance for that as the hotel officials weren't used to couples not sharing a room until their big day was behind them.

Next on the agenda was premarital counseling that we started through our church. This couple was admirably authentic. We needed that. They showed us what it was to be faithful to one another, to weather storms, to forgive, to walk in humility and how marriage is to be a testimony of Jesus and His relationship with the church. Marriage is to point people to Him, when done His way. Rob and I longed to do that.

Then, seemingly out of nowhere, a storm blew my way. I began to experience extreme anxiety. I had not encountered these symptoms before: tightness in my chest, feeling unable to breathe.

Where on earth was this coming from?! The Enemy! I was battling thoughts of inferiority to Rob. Satan began to hiss that I was tarnished and not good enough. Who are you to marry him?! He's seemingly blameless and without blemish. But, you, well... He was tormenting me with my past, and making me question if Rob and I could 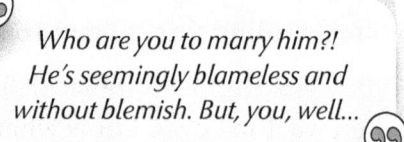 work. I wasn't sleeping. I had no appetite. And, I began to have an overwhelming, irrational fear that I had something as a result of my poor choices, years prior. So much so, that my mentor drove me to get tested. That experience was incredibly humbling, scary and unnerving as we awaited the outcome. A negative result revealed my trepidation was unreasonable and clearly a spiritual attack. Rob was by my side through it all. He could have fled and no one would have blamed him. But, again, he saw in me what I didn't yet see in myself. This battle brought to mind this verse: "For our struggle is not against flesh and blood, but against the rulers, against the authorities, against the cosmic powers of this darkness, against evil, spiritual forces in the heavens."[37]

Friend, has fear ever floored you? Like, literally taken you out for the count? Sideswiped you with a sucker punch? Gripped you with "what if?!" It's the worst, right?! You think you're journeying with Jesus, walking the narrow road, only to collide with shame. God's word says, "As far as the east is from the west, so far has he removed our transgressions from us."[38] Then, why are we berated by the lies?! Because the enemy doesn't like when we walk in our new identity as beloved sons and daughters, fully forgiven.

Satan loses his power when we walk in our purpose.

He wants to remind us of negative "remember when…" moments to keep us from stepping into a future with our good Father. But, we shouldn't be startled by his strategy. "Dear friends, don't be surprised when the fiery ordeal comes among you to test you, as if something unusual were happening to you. Instead, rejoice as you share in the sufferings of Christ, so that you may also rejoice with great joy when his glory is revealed."[39]

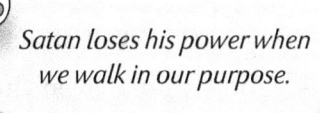

Satan loses his power when we walk in our purpose.

---

[37] Ephesians 6:12
[38] Psalm 103:12
[39] 1 Peter 4:12, 13

What I Couldn't See Before

I want His glory to be revealed even if it means me being mortified along the way.

I was learning to recognize the enemy's resistance as a reminder that he's threatened when strongholds are broken. I was learning live-time what it meant to put on the armor of God. So, the next time lies are launched our way, "Stand tall, with that belt of truth around your waist, Strap your feet with those sandals of peace, and in Every situation take up the shield of faith with which you can extinguish all the flaming arrows of the evil one. Take the helmet of salvation and the sword of the Spirit — which is the word of God. Pray at all times in the Spirit with every prayer and request, and stay alert with all perseverance and intercession for all the saints."[40]

To you, that's felt attacked like this, God will use even the most wretched parts of your story for His glory. And, you are not less than for feeling less than. Your faith isn't too small.

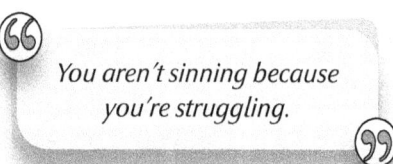
You aren't sinning because you're struggling.

You aren't sinning because you're struggling.

You can love Jesus AND be bombarded by these thoughts. To grapple with grace means you're human. Just don't grapple alone. We need people in our lives to raise our gaze when we're stuck in a stupor of shame. We need a safe soul to share our most distressing,

---

[40] Ephesians 6:14-18 (Emphasis mine)

seemingly preposterous thoughts and that person not leave, not judge and not panic when we do. There are some of you that have been fortunate enough to not experience this. So, you may not know how to help your friend or loved one during their torturous time. Please know that your presence, your staying keeps them steady, and they just need the assurance of knowing you don't think they're crazy.

This too shall pass, and they need your faith to carry theirs when they feel frantic.

And to those of us that have endured a stormy season like this, we are now equipped to empathize. Vulnerability begets vulnerability. When we meet their meltdown with "me too," they're suddenly empowered to fight the good fight. Sometimes, we may be in a space that calls for us to go first in sharing our story. In return, someone else may be incredibly relieved, knowing we've been there, and that we came out the other side, standing. Remember, we overcome the enemy by the blood of the Lamb and the word of our testimony. Our testimony can fortify others while they trek through their fiery trial. "Fight the good fight of the faith. Take hold of the eternal life to which you were called when you made your good confession in the presence of many witnesses."[41]

As I gained my bearings again, we continued to move forward with all things wedding. Next on the docket were bridal portraits. My parents came in town, I had my hair done, we had arranged

---

[41] 1 Timothy 6:12

a beautiful location to take them, only to get there and the photographer didn't show. Yep, you read that right. He didn't show. They had a family emergency, so he sent his daughter instead but without the proper equipment nor experience to ensure successful snapping. Yikes! The outcome was a letdown. They turned out just flat-out lousy. At least the wedding-moon package included pics because we needed restitution. Not long after, the day arrived for our wedding departure.

Eleven of us hopped on a plane to paradise, or so we thought. We landed in the dreamy destination of Jamaica, and we had to go thru customs/security before springing onto our shuttle for the resort. Now, I had individually wrapped an intimate undergarment for Rob to open every day while there (once married, of course.) You guys, security took great pleasure in opening Every. Single. One. to do their "due diligence," (insert eye roll) to ensure there was nothing dangerous contained inside, all while the eleven of us stood there dumbfounded by what was happening. Fortunately, someone in our party had the wherewithal to tell Rob to turn away while this played out. Can we say humiliating?! I had to giggle, or I would certainly cry. Well, you're welcome, security staff for providing amusement for your day. We couldn't get out of there fast enough.

We landed at our resorts, and the view was spectacular. We settled into our rooms and then met up for dinner. The air was salty, and our spirits were stoked. We were to marry on day three of our stay, so a mini vacay was at hand for all. We relished the sand between our toes. All was well in our world. The day before our wedding, we scheduled a snorkeling excursion. I had never been, and we were all eager. We sailed out in our little bottom-glass boat.

The waves were pretty, well, wavy, on the edge of choppy. We put our gear on and jumped in the water.

Apparently, this is supposed to be a tranquil, magical moment to soak up all the colors of the rainbow through various fish as they coast by. It didn't take long, and I drifted into the reef, which is a big no-no. Mind you, the reef contains sea urchins and oh, they're poisonous by the way. Our guide began to yell at me to get out of the reef as if I had placed myself there on purpose. So, I began to grasp onto anything I could to maneuver my way out. In the panicky process, I managed to get stung by not one but several sea urchins before I was outta there. I heaved my flustered self-back into the boat. Next stop, the nurse's corner. The news was no bueno. I'd been stung by the urchins - multiples times, my skin was seared by their stings and time would have to run its course for the poison to purge itself from my system. We were able to laugh it off and hope for the best. We made a memory, no doubt about it. The malady was manageable, and we all prepped for dinner and dancing that evening. Favorably, the night was smooth sailing. We chuckled in both our chatting and our deficiencies on the dance floor.

There's something freeing about being in a place, with the people you love, but around others you won't ever see again. We felt an increased liberty to let down our guard. With the big day the next day, we all called it a night before it was too crazy late. Little did we know, my maid of honor and I were about to have an increasingly drawn-out night.

Remember the poison from the urchins? Well, it began to eradicate itself up and out from my body. So much so, that the bathroom was my bedroom All night long. The porcelain crown was my chair, and the trashcan, my headrest. It was awful and seemed to never end until, I had no more to unload. As the sun came up, I finally felt I could lay down. Depleted and drained of all resources, I was on E for the best day of my life. Rob and I were to meet our pastor before our ceremony that morning. Rob meandered over to grab me, and he was flustered by my roommate's face at the door. She explained the enduring evening we'd had and warned him that I didn't look so peachy. I got myself together enough to go meet our minister. We were so grateful to learn that he was a follower of Jesus; therefore, he was able to honor our request for Jesus to be the center of our wedding.

Rob and I then went our separate ways to ready ourselves for the afternoon. I had to proceed with caution. I was skittish to eat anything for fear of losing it just as quick. But, I knew I needed nutrients to get me through. We managed to get hair and makeup done but not without me bolting to the bathroom on occasion. In fact, I have a priceless pic of me on the potty in my wedding dress. Again, we had to snicker, or naturally we'd cry. It was now time for bridal portraits, beachside. I got in place for my first pose and wait for it…a bird flew over and pooped on my dress. The photographer was dumbfounded. I wouldn't have believed it if I weren't living it. Unbelievable! We spot-cleaned my dress and snapped some more shots. Now the hour was here for Rob and I to assure our affections for one another in front of our party of nine. It was sweet, simple, and we all cackled when "in sickness and health" came up. The resort provided a reception in their beautiful arboretum area. Hors d'oeuvres and champagne were laid out on display. We all began to raise a glass to our future, and I gazed at Rob with angst. I was about to be sick again. I ran to the bushes nearby and let out whatever I had left in me. And this next part, well, it was horrifying.

I passed out from dehydration. It pains me to put this on paper. I was wheeled away in a wheelchair…at my freaking wedding! Rob can really laugh about this now when we tell others, but it still honestly grieves my heart. Our matrimony was mayhem. Medical staff was alerted, and an IV was suggested. No one felt comfortable with that option, being in a foreign country. So, we opted for me to drink an allotted amount of saline solution packets to rehydrate.

That night, we were supposed to have a candlelit dinner on the shore. But, needless to say, that didn't happen. Rob, bless his heart, went to dinner, at a couples only resort, alone. Alone! He was surrounded by ice sculptures but isolated by all the duos around him. He brought me back three gems: a banana, a cracker, and a cookie. I slowly sampled them all. God was still good in all of it by allowing us to have a sacred, intimate time together. The following evening, we were to enjoy our candlelit dinner that we had missed the night before. I was gaining stamina, and we were excited to dine seaside. We walked down to our table, we took our seats, the waiter placed our napkins in our lap, and out of nowhere, the biggest rush of wind blew through, knocked the tables over, and it just down poured.

I told you this chapter was a doozie!

We had to run for cover to a nearby cabana. We were beginning to think, "What the heck?! What else can go wrong?!" Well, plenty! Day three, Rob blew his eardrum out when adjusting his oxygen tank in preparation to scuba dive. The next night, we were to take a dinner cruise to a different island, but a storm blew in, and yep, canceled. Canceled!

The enemy wanted to whisper doubts about our destiny.

And honestly, we just wanted to go home at this point. The call for Texas came, and we couldn't get out of there fast enough.

We almost pulled off a flawless flight, but noooooo, let's go ahead and throw in another hurdle to the honeymoon. We were close to landing, but then we began to circle the airway. The pilot then proceeded to come on and said a storm had blown in. Shocker! Of course it did! We were unable to safely land, and we were running low on fuel. We would now have to fly to San Antonio to stop, refuel and allow the storm to subside. Mind you, this was an international flight, so no one was allowed off the plane. We parked on the tarmac for almost two hours. We had no food, and they had to send out a water truck because they were out of H2O. Everyone was hangry.

Exhausted and emotional, I began to clearly see that the enemy was afraid, of us…together. He knew that we were going to be so much more effective for the Gospel in tandem than we would be apart. He was jeopardized by our junction.

Friend, have you ever felt attacked from every angle? But, you know without a doubt that you're walking out the purposes God has for your life? This is when we must remember those fiery darts and deflect those distracting arrows.

As we finally flew back home, God granted me His penthouse perspective on our circumstances. And then, Then, I felt hopeful. I was able to call the devil's bluff and tell him to go back where he came from. While all mayhem was left unmanaged on our plane and everyone around us was complaining, we were the young newlyweds that locked arms with one another. We were a team now. If we just weathered a week like that and still came out as a couple, then we knew we were going to make it in this marriage.

So, no more taking blows from the bully with whatever he's trying to throw your way. Stand up to him and tell him where to go. He's the one that needs to cower.

Then, walk in whatever God has for you, knowing you've already won.

CHAPTER SIX REFLECTIONS

1. "Do not be anxious about anything, but in every situation, by prayer and petition, with thanksgiving, present your requests to God. And the peace of God, which transcends all understanding, will guard your hearts and your minds in Christ Jesus." Philippians 4:6-7
   How can you find peace and strength in God's presence during times of anxiety and fear?

   _____
   _____
   _____
   _____

2. "The thief comes only to steal and kill and destroy; I have come that they may have life, and have it to the full." John 10:10
   How can you still find the abundance Jesus promises when unexpected challenges arise, especially during significant moments?

   _____
   _____
   _____
   _____

3. "Put on the full armor of God, so that you can take your stand against the devil's schemes." Ephesians 6:11

   How can you recognize spiritual attacks and stand firm in your faith during those times?

   _____
   _____
   _____
   _____

4. "Therefore, as we have opportunity, let us do good to all people, especially to those who belong to the family of believers." Galatians 6:10

   In what ways can you support and encourage others when life has thrown them a curveball?

   _____
   _____
   _____
   _____

Chapter Seven

Hilltops and Valleys

When most people say, "the honeymoon's over," its dismal in nature. The blissful beginning of marriage has ceased, and reality has set in. Life has hit the fan, and challenges start to surface.

Buuuuut, quite the contrary for us. We were pleased the honeymoon was over! Did we make memories? You bet! Were they all merry, whimsical & glamorous? Ummm, no.

We could not have been happier to be home. Oh, how we missed the satisfaction of Tex-Mex. First stop after the airport, submerse ourselves in chips and salsa. Turns out, that wooed all our woes away. Who knew?!

Have you also experienced a season of ultimate anticipation only to be let down? All the hype, energy and investment into one day, one moment, one adventure. And then, it turns out to be

Nothing like you expected. If it could go wrong, it did? Ugh! Life sucks sometimes! I'm sorry things didn't pan out the way you'd hoped.

"In their hearts humans plan their course, but the Lord establishes their steps." Proverbs 16:9

When our course goes offtrack, we can still trust Who secures our steps. I know that's not easy and not without disappointment. But the longer I live, the more I believe…

when we're palms up with our plans, His purpose prevails.

Rob and I easily found ourselves loving life as a married couple. It was the simple things that brought us joy like walking our dog, working out, making dinners together, to the sacredness of sharing a bed. Life was settling in. Then, Rob soon found his schedule swamped with the X's and O's of football, and I was wrapping up my last year of college. The gridiron can often become a gridlock for marriages during football season. I had never heard the term "football widow," but I learned that many wives find themselves alone from the end of June to mid- December (if you're lucky and make the playoffs.) We were even invited to a coach's marriage retreat. Like many professions, it's a calling. The wife is a part of that calling. It takes both of you to make it work. There were Many late nights of Rob coming home…anywhere between midnight & 4 AM! Then, they'd have to be back up there on a Saturday to grade film from Friday night's game. That took pretty much all day. He'd come home and find himself conked out on the couch. I grew up playing sports, I loved competition, and I was supportive until I felt our marriage was accidentally headed the wrong direction. Rob noticed it, too. He LOVED football, and honestly, was on a fast track to be a head coach one day. We had to sit down and ask the Lord if that's what He wanted for our marriage. We were both willing and ready to walk that out if we felt confirmation from the Lord, but we didn't. In our gut, we knew He had something different for us. There's no doubt that Rob shared the love of Jesus with others while coaching and would have continued, but we sensed the invitation to something new.

Simultaneously, Rob's principal called out leadership and administrative strengths in him and saw principal potential. We submitted that idea to the Lord, and He was calling us to a change.

Our second year of marriage, we chose to sell the home we had only briefly lived in and transitioned to an apartment. Rob was going back to school! We had diligently worked to pay off our student loans, and we didn't want to find ourselves indebted again. So, the funds from our sell would allow Rob to pursue and pay for his master's along the way. I had graduated by then, and I landed a job with his school district. I wasn't using my degree. But, we had all holidays off and extended weekends together during the summers. That was invaluable! This time together was priority since we knew he would be incredibly busy with work and going back to school. I also found a side job where I could work on Saturdays to help us stay out of debt. We were committed to our next steps.

This was life as we knew it, and we couldn't have been happier. We visited a couple of churches in the midst, and we landed right where God wanted us for that season. We grew in friendship with other couples and did life together.

Fast forward two years. Rob graduated, and we were pregnant with our 1st child. We were extremely blessed that Rob landed a job at a local high school within our district, and he was pumped to start this new chapter. We were also humbled to conceive so quickly. We did not take for granted that some struggle to do so. During my pregnancy, however, I began to experience inflammation, redness, swelling, pain & stiffness in my hands and feet that seemingly came out of nowhere. We consistently worked out a few nights a week for years, even while dating. But, the discomfort became debilitating. It hurt to walk. We didn't understand what was happening. I mentioned it to my dr. He gently said in passing that he was concerned I may have rheumatoid arthritis, but that there was nothing we could do during pregnancy. Then, a dreadful day dawned. I started spotting. We prayed, we believed, we hoped, we continued our day but cautiously. We even went to a Sunday School function, hoping for the best. As we made our way home, I knew something wasn't right. We took the steps up to our apartment with dread. To my fellow friend that's experienced this, you know the worst was upon me. We quickly had to triage the trauma.

I came out with quiet tears, and Rob knew. We made our way to the hospital. We waited and waited and waited some more. They finally got us back and took us for a sonogram. Our hearts stopped as no heartbeat was found. We could see our baby, but our baby would never see us.

Shocked. Stunned. Speechless. The sonographer gave us a moment to sit in the still of our sadness. This happened on a Saturday, so we were sent home to follow up with our doctor on Monday. Monday came, and he said I needed a Dilation &

Curettage procedure (D&C) to ensure everything had passed and to best prepare my body to try again.

Grievously, miscarriages can be a common occurrence for women.

I want to sit with you in your sorrow. For your loss, for your wounds, for your tears, your heartache, your confusion, for your hopes and dreams that have not come to pass...yet.

To my dear friend, that feels like your heart can't handle the hurt...

> *I want to sit with you in your sorrow.*

I
AM
SO
SORRY

I'm sorry that your world was wrecked in a flash. This incident left us swirling in a whirlwind of emotions. Our hearts were geared up for growth & new life but instead, we mourned that loss of life that we had the painful privilege to carry, if even for a short while. We lamented the long nights we wouldn't have & the stretch marks we wouldn't see.

What I Couldn't See Before

Still in the middle of our mourning, the doctor wanted to run some tests to see if we could determine the cause. He also said it was time to test for rheumatoid arthritis. The results came in. I did, in fact, have RA. And not just RA, but the most aggressive form. We experienced the loss of life in our baby and now, loss of life as we knew it.

I began the multi-stage process of grieving. Denying what had just happened was well, undeniable. But, denying the diagnosis of an incurable, autoimmune disease? I didn't want to face the facts. I had been justifying my aches and pains to be old sports injuries. That made sense, right? Until it didn't. When the palms of my hands and the bottoms of my feet were red, feverish and incredibly painful, I couldn't exactly chalk it up to a torn ligament or a broken bone from years past. And, for crying out loud, I was only twenty-five! I was shocked by our circumstances.

At this juncture, I did not struggle with anger towards God. I wasn't mad at Him, didn't feel short-changed by Him or anything of the like. I was realizing that I was angry with myself. Yep, the enemy jumped on that train quick! The poor choices of my past crept back up, and I became consumed by regret. I was on a quest to know why I had RA, what I did to cause it. Satan started to sway me towards self-condemnation, and that seemed to answer my "why." I pondered the poison that this was punishment for my waywardness, and now it was my time to pay - through pain.

Those pensive thoughts led to bargaining.

God, I'm so sorry for my rebellious routine in my younger days. I'm sorry I knew better, but I didn't choose better. I'm sorry I didn't listen to your nudges in the 90's. I'm sorry I caused my parents so much grief and sleepless nights. I'm sorry that I didn't want to do things Your way, that I wandered wildly in high school. I'm sorry I was having too much "fun" to follow you. I'm sorry I claimed to be a Christian, but I certainly didn't act like one. Please God, please! Please say it isn't so! I've been all in with You for years now. Remember, You grabbed my attention that dark, unfortunate night in high school, and I was sobered by my sin. . .

The symptoms stayed, and my heart was broken. B R O K E N! All my life, I had been a competitor, an athlete, a go-getter. I could no longer walk across the room without shoes on. My hands just ached with anguish for no causable reason. I remember calling Rob from work one day, quietly crying because my stinkin' elbow hurt so freaking bad! The loss of mobility was emotionally excruciating.

Go for a quick jog? Nope, not gonna happen.

A swift circuit of weights? No.

Play basketball with Rob at his school gym? A torturing no.

Turn your neck to look at Rob? Painfully, no.

Easily pick up a full glass of water without my hand giving way to the mysterious weakness? Still no.

One day, just a few years prior (pre-diagnosis,) Rob and I were visiting my parents. We had all loaded up to go to dinner. We got down the road, and Rob and I realized that we had forgotten something at my mom and dad's house. We spontaneously told them to let us out right there, that we'd run home and be back at that same spot before they got back from running an errand. Game on! My parents left us there and made their way to the mall for a quick purchase. Rob and I ran back to the house, got our item and darted back out the door. That sounds so silly, but it was exhilarating! We were free. We didn't realize how very free we were.

And, sure enough, we beat them back to our meeting spot. I missed the freedom of that spontaneity and physicality.

Treatment for RA? Medication. But, the caveat was no meds while in the mother-bearing stage. It did cross our minds that adoption may need to be a consideration after our miscarriage and now this. We had come to terms with the diagnosis and accepting it was necessary in order to move forward. We didn't know what the future foretold. But, we were willing and ready to try and conceive again.

So, we put a pin on treating the RA for the time being and by the grace of God, we got pregnant fairly soon. This time around, I required a daily shot in my abdomen, every day for thirty-four weeks to ensure proper blood supply traveled to the baby. And, you know what? My RA went into remission during this pregnancy!! I felt great! A few weeks after the injection regimen ceased, it was medically necessary to commence our baby's arrival into this world. An induction was scheduled just 4 days before due date. Labor was laborious and painful but slowly progressing. The time came to push. We did not find out what we were having, so we were anticipating the best surprise of our lives. Our baby came, and our doctor calmly told Rob to turn the recorder off, he motioned to the nurse and before we knew it, there were about six more medical personnel in there and we had barely caught a glimpse of our baby. It was a GIRL! Our precious baby girl had made her way. But, the cord was wrapped around her neck, and she was not breathing. Hence, the team of people that swooped in. She had already left the room before we knew what was going on. Since she was our firstborn, we honestly were slightly oblivious to what was actually happening due to the incredibly composed staff. Was this normal protocol after delivery? They were tight-lipped at first but very reassuring, so we were peaceful.

Our daughter was placed in NICU. She was born with four holes in her lungs, known as spontaneous pneumothorax. We had not held her nor seen her yet. She was placed in a 100% oxygen cube and would be there for five days, in hopes that the holes would close up on their own. After she was settled, they allowed us to go see and hold her for the first time. But, holding her was only allowed for me to feed her, and then she needed to be placed right back in her oxygen cube. It was heartbreaking that we couldn't hold her and be with her as we wanted to.

We are eternally grateful that her lungs healed up on their own, and we were able to take the daughter of our dreams home. After arriving at our apartment, our newfound church crew blessed us with over 2 weeks of meals. We were blown away! We had only met this group once, and they lavished us with love. The first six months with her were blissful. I recall many occasions when I would just break down and tears fell down my face as I read her a nursery rhyme, held her, stared at her, sang to her. The love I had for her was overwhelming.

I LOVED BEING A MOM, and I still do.

I was soon overwhelmed by something else. The pain and symptoms of RA returned with a roar. I quickly found myself struggling terribly to button the little clasps on her onesie or pull the tabs to on her diaper. Some days, unbuckling her car seat felt impossible. The little things became big obstacles. I scheduled an appointment with my rheumatologist, and might I add, he had no bedside manner. Compassion was not on his job description. It was time to have the unavoidable conversation about medicine.

What I Couldn't See Before

This medicine was also given to cancer patients as well as for other alarming reasons. It was imperative that I stop nursing. I mourned that this chapter of motherhood was ending. But, I chose to be grateful for the six months I was able to do so. My joints were so swollen and inflamed that I needed steroids to calm them down. Many refer to this med as the monster medicine because it has potential to put you on edge, cause weight gain and prevent sleeping. For me, it was a mend to my misery. I had a love/hate relationship with it. This brought us relief and time as we pursued whatever we could to avoid the other medication.

I eliminated this food, that product and those ingredients. We ordered supplements. I fasted. I tried a special cream. I went to a chiropractor. I squeezed in trips for physical therapy and custom splints for both wrists in the interim. I went forward for prayer at church, time after time. I was anointed with oil. I read books. I got a 2nd opinion.

I continued to surmise that this must be my fault and that I was being punished. I deserved it.

Why is it that I struggled with these thoughts towards myself? This notion did not even cross my mind for someone else's strife. I could easily extend compassion and grace to others, but I failed to receive His grace for me. Furthermore, self-compassion wasn't even in my vocabulary at this point. We snatched at anything to alleviate symptoms. We fought and tried any and every option. We were desperate to eliminate this disease, and our hearts' longing was to avoid medication due to the possible side effects.

We exhausted ourselves & our resources by running from reality.

Friend, have you been there? In denial about your trial? Angry at anyone, someone, everyone? Determined to make a trade for your torture? So hungry for healing?

No matter the pain, it can bring us to our knees. It's important to lament the long-suffering in order to move forward. And, I wish I could say that we can pray our problems away. Or, that belief minus doubt = breakthrough. But, sometimes we fall flat on our face and find ourselves empty-handed, with no answers nor solutions. How on earth can this be good, God?! Your Word says nothing is impossible with You.

We wrestle and worry, but could it be that this is all part of our story? For our good, the good of others and His glory?

Let's revisit Jacob's journey with God in Genesis 32. Jacob spent his life running, hiding, buying out or manufacturing his own blessing and later found himself scuffling for God's grace, in the middle of the night. Parts of Jacob's story weren't pretty and poised, were they? But, Jacob didn't realize that God wanted to bless him all along. Sadly, he had an identity problem. He lived as an orphan, not a beloved son. He was full of fear; therefore, he sought to control his circumstances. Sound familiar? Yikes, my hand's sheepishly going up. Yep, been there.

Jacob was quite audacious in the wrestle as he told God, "I will not let you go unless you bless me."[42]

---

[42] Genesis 32:26

Could it be that the blessing comes FROM the wrestle? And, is it possible that the blessing will look very different than we imagine? Yes and yes.

For now, we wrestle through our grief until we come to a place of surrender. And surrender, well, that's where we learn to trust Him even when we can't see Him at work. The surrender involves coming to terms with what we hoped would be, laying it at His feet with apprehension and then doing our part to follow Him through the disappointment.

> *Could it be that the blessing comes FROM the wrestle?*

God gives us the courage to take reality by the reigns as He carries us thru the hard.

We were cornered by our circumstances. My body needed medicine. So, medicine we took. And, the wrestle continued. The medicine prevented me from being able to taste food. So, I lost interest in eating and lost weight I didn't have to lose. We transitioned to injections, and that did the trick. You better believe I enjoyed my food after that. Tex-Mex saved the day again. We were beginning to find hope in the hard. My gaze lifted, and my gait improved. I continued to love motherhood through it all, and I adored this gift of a girl He had given us. Her face, y'all.

The tears, they continued to spontaneously flow as I was struck by her, which was often.

Friend, what do you need to grieve? Or, what do you need to face in order to grieve it? May I encourage you, wrestle through the grief. Has it been stuffed down? Are you in denial that it's even there? Do you need to make that dreadful call to the doctor? Do you need to propose counseling to your spouse? Do You need counseling? I'd like to say that I'll sit with you on your couch while you grieve, while you tackle your turn of events, but I have something even better. The Holy Spirit is already in the room with you.

And, let me say this: This diagnosis doesn't define you! Whatever the broken thing is, it is not your identity. YOU are not broken. YOU are a beloved child of God. Let's wrestle with God until the blessing comes. I know you're afraid. I was, too. I know you don't want this. Man, life can be savage sometimes. But, may I also say that it's time. Make the call, confess the cry of your heart, shed the tears in the shower. You can do hard things. You can do this hard thing of facing your fear, laying down that disappointment and letting go. Let Him hold you in this hard.

CHAPTER SEVEN REFLECTIONS

1. "Blessed are those who mourn, for they shall be comforted." Matthew 5:4

   What do you need to face and grieve? Don't be afraid of the silence. Ask the Holy Spirit to show you, and He will.

   _____
   _____
   _____
   _____

2. "He gives strength to the weary and increases the power of the weak." Isaiah 40:29

   What is one step you can take to productively process your grief? Let one person know so that they can help you.

   _____
   _____
   _____
   _____

3. "Give thanks in all circumstances; for this is God's will for you in Christ Jesus." 1 Thessalonians 5:18

   How can you find joy and gratitude in the simple moments of life, even amid challenges?

   _____
   _____
   _____
   _____

4. "Cast all your anxiety on him because he cares for you." 1 Peter 5:7

   How can you surrender your pain to God and trust Him with your healing and future?

   _____
   _____
   _____
   _____

Chapter Eight

Paralyzed by Panic

Life was good and sweet and simple. Harleigh and I had dates to the library for story-time, the park, and walks to feed the neighborhood horses and donkey with our dog, Max. The little things were, and continue to be, my favorite. Snuggles in the LaZBoy, painting in the driveway, tea parties & carpet picnics while watching her favorite show. Those days with her before our family grew were treasured and meaningful.

The day came when we were ready to expand our family. I was doing really well. We felt the timing was optimal for me to get off RA meds to try for another baby. I'm sad to say that we had another loss of pregnancy before we were able to conceive again. We weren't as far into this pregnancy as our first miscarriage. No D&C required. We mourned this loss, but it honestly motivated us to try, try again. We got pregnant soon after. Things were very different this time around. No daily injections were needed, and we were grateful. But, RA reared its ugly head with wrath. It set up camp in my shoulder the most. The pain was so intense that it kept me up at night. I was doing my best to not take anything for the pain for the health of the baby. Ice and the recliner became my default. I was learning to just live with it.

One evening, Rob was at a school event, and Harleigh and I were walking Max. I was twenty-six weeks (about six months) pregnant. My stomach started cramping terribly. Fear fueled me to get home fast. After a call to the doctor, I called Rob to tell him I was on my way to the ER. A friend met me there and took Harleigh with her. Rob hurried to the hospital. I was having contractions, and I was quickly sent to labor & delivery. They gave me an injection that would hopefully stop them. It worked. I also had the opportunity to explain the pain I was experiencing in my shoulder and the lack of sleep as a result. They stressed the importance of sleep for the baby's development, so they temporarily put me on something for sleep in order for my body to rest.

The contractions ceased, so we were sent home to lay low. We were referred to a specialist to help me manage the RA while pregnant. While we sought to avoid medicine, we had to come to terms that the stress of RA being out of control was potentially detrimental to the baby, as well. The specialist came up with a conservative plan that would bring me relief. The last stretch of the pregnancy was far better than the outset.

I went into labor without induction, and our second child arrived on their due date. We were able to ride this one out. We had a healthy baby boy! And there were no complications for either one of us. All went so smoothly that we were able to go home the next day. We were excited to be home as a family of four.

Five weeks postpartum, and it was time to see my rheumatologist. We changed doctors to one with a dose of compassion. Man am I glad we did! My RA numbers were terribly high, and it was aggressive. The doctor told me I needed to stop nursing in a week and that I needed to get on not one but two different injections to attack this quickly. I had not been on one of the meds yet, and I was panicky. The potential side effects were petrifying. He also put me in touch with an orthopedic surgeon because my shoulder was in bad shape.

I found myself at another crossroads. Would I trust God with these circumstances, or would I choose the delusion of control? As if fretting and fighting reality were a solid way of handling this hardship! I was wrestling once again. I DID NOT want to take this medication. I DID NOT want to stop nursing and abruptly at that. I DID NOT want to see a surgeon for my shoulder. We had an infant and a two-year-old to tend to. The mom guilt was a gauntlet, friends. Keep in mind that postpartum hormones were also in high gear.

I was able to stop nursing in that seven-day period but not without tears, heartache and the physical discomfort of wearing cabbage leaves in my bra to help dry my supply short. The night came when our son was to have his first bottle. I realize that some moms are unable to nurse from the beginning, or others opt out for different reasons. But, when you long to provide that for your child, and you're physically capable but you're told to stop for your own health, it's devastating. The skin-to-skin contact, losing yourself in their gaze, the connection you feel with your child is beyond matchless in moments. I fed him his first bottle as the tears quietly fell. I realized that Rob was able to start bonding with him through bottle feeds, too. I know that was a gift, but goodness gracious my heart was disappointed.

My mom came into town to see the orthopedic surgeon with me while Rob stayed with the kids. I had to get an injection with dye for the x-ray and then an MRI. The dye would help them see clearly. For those of you that have had an MRI before, you know. If you weren't claustrophobic before, you certainly were coming out. A very confined space, you can't move, and the loud knocking starts to wear on your last nerve. After multiple scans, the doctor basically said my shoulder had been eaten alive by the RA, and that I needed a shoulder replacement. I'm sorry, what did you say?! Ummmm, No. The pain was poignant, but I was not about to have surgery and be out for months of rehab with two very small littles at home. And I wasn't even 30! So, he gave me an injection, and I went on my way. The shot sent solace to my shoulder. I was grateful for the reprieve, but now our focus was to turn to these meds I didn't want to manage. The cost alone was reason enough to panic. Over $1,300 for one shot, one month's worth. Fortunately, co-pay assistance was offered, and that narrowed the cost to a feasible amount.

It honestly blows my mind how drugs that are required for people's livelihood are so preposterously priced. Yet, someone can pay…I don't know, $1.68 for a month's supply of pain medication, a mere band aid to the person's problems. It's outrageous, and the system needs some hope.

I digress.

As Rob and I began to do my 1st set of injections from home, we had to submit and entrust our fears to the Lord. My prayer became, "God, please protect me from potential harm from this medicine, and please use it for my good." Deep breath in, "I will not be afraid." Deep breath out, "For You are with me."

Have you prayed a similar prayer? Faced circumstances where neither option A nor B were ideal? Sometimes, we just must do the thing afraid, huh? Let's take a moment and do those prayer breaths together.

Deep breath in,
"God, I will not be afraid _____ (tell Him your fear.)"
Now, deep breath out,
"For You are with me."

The honest truth is that when you are stripped of self-sufficiency, the pride peels back. Part of your dignity dies, but that's actually to your advantage. There's no room for pretense, and you begin to realize that you need God. That's a gift that will keep on giving. There are many out there that don't see their need for Jesus. They're seemingly successful in every way, but their souls are shallow and idle. When faced with discomfort, no matter the kind, the idol of comfort gets crushed. Who knew that was an idol?! To be vulnerable and humble is a posture you learn to embrace when your circumstances feel out of control. And there is a softening that occurs...if you let it. Likewise, when you're sidelined from the seemingly simple and small tasks of life, you develop a deep appreciation for things you once took for granted.

What I Couldn't See Before

Now, I'd like to say that this next part began the road to recovery. One could argue that maybe it did. But, I took a major detour. I started the new medicine, but I was held captive by crushing concern. In fact, the fear grew despite my efforts to meditate on Scripture and pour out my prayers. Unfortunately, one of my fears came to fruition from the meds. I developed a staph infection. I had to come off the RA meds and then on antibiotics to rid of the staph. After two weeks of treatment, I started having the craziest reactions. My neck became terribly red & hot, then it started traveling all the way down my body. The next day, we ended up in urgent care.

We did not know what was happening! Turns out, I was allergic to the sulfa that was in the antibiotics. I have never itched and scratched so obsessively in all my life. For days following, I would wake and have some newfound oddity as a reaction. One day, I had a black eye, the next, a giant upper lip, the next, an incredibly large, lower lip. All in the name of that reaction working its way out. It was terrible and honestly, laughable. But this interruption only fueled my fear of being on the meds. Once I resumed RA treatment, I was having moments throughout the day where I'd go in our closet, drop to my knees and beg of the Lord to take away my dismay, change my thinking, to please make it stop. I know this isn't so, but it seemed the more I tried to lean on the Lord, my angst thickened. I was continually reciting back to myself, "Trust in the Lord with all your heart and lean not on your own understanding; in all your ways submit to Him, and He will make your paths straight."[43]

---

[43] Proverbs 3:5,6

My road was quite warped though. A war was being waged. Simultaneously, while trying to be mama to two littles, my symptoms were still present. It would take up to three months before the medicine worked its magic. One time, I had to have my foot x-rayed. It was so incredibly swollen and painful, that I was sure it was broken. Nope, Radically Aggressive RA put me in a boot for a week after an injection on the bony, top part of my foot was given for the inflammation.

Rob was just starting his new role as the principal of a middle school, and sleep was imperative for him. He was putting in a lot of hours in preparation for the new year. In the middle of the night, I would bolt upright, gasp for air, sweating, all of my limbs were numb and I felt like my heart was pounding. I was having panic attacks, but my mind was playing dirty tricks on me. I was irrationally convinced that something was terribly wrong as a result of the new medication. This went on for days, and I wasn't telling Rob. I did not want to add stress to his already stressful role.

My attempts to spare Rob from my turmoil ceased at the worst time possible! My mental meltdown spewed up and out on the first day of school for him and his students. Worst timing ever, right?! I'm glad you agree. I had been trying so very hard to tame the torment, but I was utterly exhausted and overwhelmed. I couldn't do it anymore. I felt paralyzed by my panic. So, with brokenness in my voice, I made the call to Rob. . . remember, it was his first day of school. He was home before I knew it. His concern was heavy for both the kids and me. Fortunately, he had a great team at work that stepped up. My mind was unwell. I could not stop the soundtrack of fear that refused to shuffle with other life-giving notes. Nope, fear was on repeat in my head. My OB/GYN walked closely with me through all of it. He was wonderful, and he understood the mental/emotional struggle that the physical realities of RA (or any chronic pain) brought with it. He had journeyed with me through it all and told me that If I need help via meds, for a season, they were available. At this moment, all ego (whatever was left of it) could do was exit. I needed help in a big way. I called my OB/GYN, and he put me on a low dose of anxiety medication.

> *I want to take a moment to speak life into Your darkness of despair.*
> *You don't have to do this alone.*
> *You are not failing.*
> *This is not your fault.*
> *It's ok to ask for help.*
> *It's ok to not be okay.*
> *Shame is a liar.*
> *You did not cause this.*
> *You are no less a Jesus follower because you fell prey to panic.*
> *Your prayers are not pointless.*
> *Anxiety and depression does not negate your calling.*
> *You may be in a mess, but you are not a mess.*
> *God is with you, even when He seems sequestered.*

> *You are capable.*
>
> *You are brave.*
>
> *You are worthy.*
>
> *You are resilient.*
>
> *Let others in.*
>
> *Jesus promises to work this very thing for your good.*
>
> *Your prayers have power, even if sheer sighs.*
>
> *You will get through this.*
>
> *You are strong for seeking support.*
>
> *Better days are ahead.*
>
> *Jesus has more for you.*

I am immensely grateful that so much ground has been taken for mental health. The stigma that's been stamped on this issue is truly becoming a smudge of the past. Thank God! There is no shame in needing help. Fifteen years ago, though, it still held the perception that one lacked faith when mentally struggling. It was unmentionable. In fact, I reached out for Godly counsel during this, and I was simply told to hunker down and have more faith. Once more, I wrestled with the Lord. Was my faith fractured even though I was doing all the "right" things and yet, I was still struggling? No. The answer is no for you, too.

What I Couldn't See Before

We can have faith as small as a mustard seed, and yet, the mountain remains.

That doesn't mean we've failed. Waiting on God can often feel like we're wandering aimlessly in the wilderness though, right?"

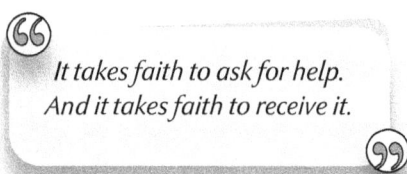

It takes faith to ask for help. And it takes faith to receive it.

It takes faith to ask for help. And it takes faith to receive it. I had been in a pit of despair, and I could not reason my way out. The anxiety medication was an arm extended to get me back on track. My qualms quieted. What once felt relentless had been released from my mind. We were thankful. The downside though is that I couldn't really feel anything. My emotions felt numb. It's like I'd want to cry, but it was the strangest thing. I couldn't. Happy or sad tears. I did not like that part, but I recognized the need for it in the interim in order to get me on the other side. This would be temporary, but it was necessary. This was a season. I held onto hope that another season would come. "There is a time for everything, and a season for every activity under the heavens."[44]

In all of that, life carried on as usual with two littles. We still made trips to the library, had those carpet picnics and now our little guy could enjoy tummy time while our sweet girl danced or watched Abby on Sesame Street. We enjoyed days of making homemade applesauce and homemade chocolate pie with our daughter, pushed up to the stove top on her chair. Story-time snuggles and trips to the zoo. Football games, pumpkin patches and visits to Santa. Springtime swinging and summertime at the splash pad. Life was still good in all of it. I refused to be paralyzed

---

[44] Ecclesiastes. 3:1

by chronic pain nor let it steal from my family any more than it already had.

I began to find healthy again, and I was able to wean off anxiety meds. The RA meds had really kicked in, and I began to feel great. Like, really, really great.

Friends, when faced with difficult decisions to make, whatever that decision may be, it's important to count the cost on both sides. Doctors were quick to inform me of potential side effects to watch out for with plenty of resources to scare you out of moving forward. It's awful! I still mute the source if an advertisement comes on for medicine. After hearing that, who on earth would willingly raise their hand and say, "Me. I'd like to start taking said medicine. I cannot wait to get started. I've been looking forward to this day for so long."

Said. No. One. Ever.

But, what they don't say or hadn't yet was the cost of not taking medicine. The risks of not managing your symptoms (physical or mental) and keeping the havoc at bay. So, while said medicine may be scary, can I please encourage you to count the cost of not taking it? Sometimes, it takes more faith to take the medicine than not to.

Whatever you are in the middle of, please consider both perspectives. I know that we want to pray our problems away, but sometimes it doesn't play out precisely. I believe our God is Big. I believe He wants us to prosper. I believe He can perform miracles and still does. I believe He's compassionate. I believe that He grieves when we do.

But, He's also a mystery. I do not understand Him, but maybe that's not our assignment. 1 Corinthians 13:9-10 says, "For we know in part and we prophesy in part, but when completeness comes, what is in part disappears." I find so much encouragement from those verses! On this earth, we only get a glimpse of what is happening from our limited landscape. We can lose ourselves in the "why." At times, His grace allows us to see but often, we're called to trust the mystery of His goodness especially when circumstances seem less than "good." We don't have the whole story! One day though, "in part" will be no more.

We get to partner with God in stewarding our bodies, our minds and our decisions and that requires wisdom. We pursue Him through prayer, His word and Godly relationships. When we seek out doctors, therapists, specialists or advisors that love God and want to serve Him by helping others, we can submit their counsel to the Lord. Then, we trust Him with whatever the decision is that needs to be walked out. We don't have to like it, and we probably won't. Trust is a choice not a feeling, but God made professionals. He places them in our lives to help us.

By calling on outside resources for help, our faith is not diminished.

Let's go back to Ecclesiastes 3 for a minute.

"There is a time for everything, and a season for every activity under the heavens:

a time to be born and a time to die, a time to plant and a time to uproot, a time to kill and a time to heal, a time to tear down and a time to build, a time to weep and a time to laugh, a time to mourn and a time to dance, a time to scatter stones and a time to gather them, a time to embrace and a time to refrain from embracing, a time to search and a time to give up, a time to keep and a time to throw away, a time to tear and a time to mend, a time to be silent and a time to speak, a time to love and a time to hate, a time for war and a time for peace."[45]

King Solomon confirms for us that seasons come and seasons go. Whatever you are in is a season. A season with no end in sight? Quite possibly, but this will not last for the rest of forever, I promise. I know it may feel that way, but feelings are fickle when life is fragile.

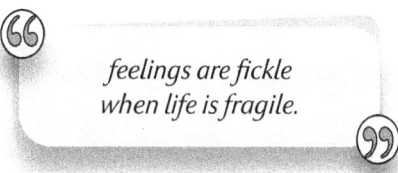
feelings are fickle when life is fragile.

As I reflect on this season, it makes me think of the time when the Israelites were fleeing Egypt. Track with me here.

Pharoah had agreed to let them go, but then he and his men were on the pursuit to bring them back to bondage. The Israelites saw them coming. They cried out to the Lord, and they lamented to Moses. They questioned the goodness of God. They were fretting, they didn't know what to do. They were even so bold to tell Moses that they wished they had just stayed in Egypt in slavery. All they could see were the hundreds of men and chariots with their backs seemingly against the wall, excuse me, the sea.

They did not know the whole story.

Next, "Moses answered the people, "Do not be afraid. Stand firm and you will see the deliverance the Lord will bring you today. The Egyptians you see today you will never see again."[46] He goes on…

"The Lord will fight for you; you need only to be STILL."[47]

---

[45] Ecclesiastes 3:1-8
[46] Exodus 14:13
[47] Exodus 14:14 (emphasis mine)

What I Couldn't See Before

The VERY next verse states, "Then the Lord said to Moses, "Why are you crying out to me? Tell the Israelites to MOVE on."[48]

The Israelites were told to be still and then move in two verses. They went from mourning to dancing. These verses give me a tremendous amount of hope. They were in and out of a season before they knew it. I know, I know, they later found themselves in a season that seemingly never ended. But we're not gonna go there right now.

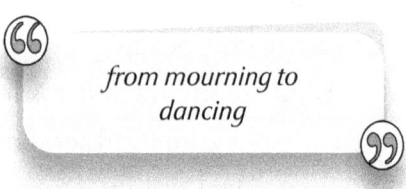

from mourning to dancing

Friend, what season do you find yourself in? Are you fretting, toiling, striving to amend your situation? If so, will you let Him fight for you and you need only to be still?

Or are you sitting on your spiritual loins, and He's calling you to courage? It may be time to move, friend. When we seek the Lord to be set free from bondage, we can't forget to remember that the Pharaoh of today will attempt to hunt us down. It may appear that we have nowhere to run or stay, but oh, we do. And the remedy may look like unraveling before the healing. We may even crave those shackles when the resistance gets stronger. And it will get stronger.

But the buzzer will go off on this period of pain. A new season will come.

---

[48] Exodus 14:15

CHAPTER EIGHT REFLECTIONS

1. "He says, "Be still, and know that I am God." Ps. 46:10
   What season are you in right now?
   Is it one that God is inviting you to just be still?
   OR
   "Have I not commanded you? Be strong and courageous. Do not be afraid; do not be discouraged, for the Lord your God will be with you wherever you go." Joshua 1:9
   Are you in a season where He's calling you to move?

   _____
   _____
   _____
   _____

2. "Trust in the Lord with all your heart and lean not on your own understanding; in all your ways submit to Him, and He will make your paths straight." Proverbs 3:5-6
   What steps can I take to seek Godly counsel and trust God with difficult decisions I'm currently facing?

   _____
   _____
   _____
   _____

3. "There is no fear in love. But perfect love drives out fear, because fear has to do with punishment. The one who fears is not made perfect in love." 1 John 4:18

   What fear(s) do you need to lay down and let your Heavenly Father lavish you with His perfect love?

   _____
   _____
   _____
   _____

4. "Two are better than one, because they have a good return for their labor: If either of them falls down, one can help the other up." Ecclesiastes 4:9-10

   How can you support and encourage your spouse or loved ones during challenging seasons, ensuring you stay united and strong?

   _____
   _____
   _____
   _____

5. "Is anyone among you sick? Let them call the elders of the church to pray over them and anoint them with oil in the name of the Lord." James 5:14

   Is there an invitation for you to humble yourself and seek out leadership in your church or faith community to ask for prayer on your behalf?

   _____
   _____
   _____
   _____

Chapter Nine

Don't Fold on Your Faith

Rob and I were so happy to put a period on our pain. The elimination of our agony freed us up for ministry. We began hosting young, single adults at our house, and it was a blast! They brought so much life, and their confidence in the goodness of God was contagious. During this, we took a leap of faith and decided to rent out our existing home rather than sell it. There were lots of nerves involved (mostly mine), but we felt this was a good opportunity for our future. Our first tenant was actually a single mom that was able to provide a room for the first time, for each of her girls. We were able to pray over them, bless them and experience God's goodness for ourselves in that provision. It was such a blessing for both parties.

All that said, we decided to make the move just down the street from Rob's school where he was the principal. Our singles' group was such a gift. They all pitched in and were tremendous in helping us make that transition. It was a privilege to do life with them. Rob and I intended to make this home for quite some time. We envisioned our kids attending the elementary school, a stone's throw from him. We even talked about the advantages of Dad being their principal one day. Middle school is a lot to manage, and they'd have the freedom to run into Dad's office at any time for a quick hug and be on their way. Whew! They'd be in good hands.

We had momentum! Momentum in our marriage, our family, ministry, work and health. We were basking in His kindness towards us. We were plugged in and passionate with How God was moving in our church and our lives. Our faith was fortified, and we were eager to see what God had next. So much so, we sought counsel, and they affirmed that it was good timing to stop meds and position ourselves for a miracle. I made an appointment with my doctor to discuss our desire. As a physician, he thought we were fools. As a fellow believer in the God of miracles, he understood. He even told me of another patient that drove to a specific church out of state to seek prayer for healing, and her prayers had been answered. Healing had happened. He knew it was possible. He'd now witnessed the supernatural in one woman, and we shared the same faith for mine. At this juncture, he knew it didn't matter that he had MD after his name because he knew the One who had A.D. after His. Jesus died for our freedom. "But He was pierced for our transgressions, He was crushed for our iniquities; the punishment that brought us peace was on Him, and by His wounds we are healed."[49]

I still remember the conflicted expression on my doctor's face. It's like he was battling the facts that he knew of RA and the truth

---

[49] Isaiah 53:5

of what Jesus said in Mark 9:23, "Everything is possible for one who believes." I could see it in his eyes. He echoed the prayer, "I do believe; help me overcome my unbelief."[50]

Faith feels feebleminded to the world, but in reality, "it's confidence in what we hope for and assurance about what we do not see."[51]

Have you ever dared to detour and put all your money on God rather than man? Pushed all the chips in to cash in on faith? Desperate for a Holy remedy? Whether we're asking God to mend our marriage, alleviate our ailments, pursue the prodigal or propagate a pregnancy, we crave for His hand alone to craft the cure. We're longing to hear from Jesus, "Woman, you have great faith! Your request is granted." "And her daughter was healed in that moment."[52] OR, "When Jesus heard this, He was amazed and said to those following Him, "Truly I tell you, I have not found anyone in Israel with such great faith." "Then Jesus said to the centurion, "Go! Let it be done just as you believed it would." "And his servant was healed at that moment."[53] Yes, Lord! Let it be so in our lives, too!

---

[50] Mark 9:24
[51] Hebrews 11:1
[52] Matthew 15:28
[53] Matthew 8: 10, 13

What I Couldn't See Before

Rob and I believed in the impossible, and we craved the inconceivable. We intended to eliminate medicine so that Jehovah-Jireh, the Lord will provide, would be our only justification for healing. Therefore, we got off the meds and got on our knees. I went forward at church to be anointed with oil, prayer and petition. "Is anyone among you sick? Let them call the elders of the church to pray over them and anoint them with oil in the name of the Lord. And the prayer offered in faith will make the sick person well; the Lord will raise them up. If they have sinned, they will be forgiven. Therefore, confess your sins to each other and pray for each other so that you may be healed. The prayer of a righteous person is powerful and effective."[54]

We confessed with courage while also crying out, "Search me, God, and know my heart; test me and know my anxious thoughts. See if there is any offensive way in me and lead me in the way everlasting."[55]

And then, we waited. We watched for God to move. "I wait for the Lord, my whole being waits, and in His word, I put my hope."[56] We persistently plead for prayer from church and close connections. We anticipated the arrival of our miracle. Two, long months passed, and our window of waiting was waning. Time was not in our corner. "Have more faith," we were told. "It's coming."

Our waiting turned to weeping.

Healing didn't happen. The enemy wanted us to feel like fools. RA symptoms started to surface, and I felt stupid. "How far did your faith get you now?" spewed Satan. I was mortified for missing

---

[54] James 5:14-16
[55] Psalm 139:23, 24
[56] Psalm 130:5

out on the miraculous. Back to my doctor I went. Honestly, my heart hurt worse for people like my doctor who desperately wanted to believe alongside me. Somehow, I feared his faith, or those like him, would be fractured since wholeness didn't work out. "God, don't you want these people to believe in You?! You're not doing Yourself any favors here."

I had to remind myself that, "Hope does not disappoint, because the love of God has been poured out in our hearts by the Holy Spirit, who was given to us."[57]

Nevertheless, I was dreadfully disappointed.

You too?

"Why God why?" we ask.

Friend, I am so very sorry that your sorrow swelled, and now you're in need of more mending than you initially set out for. I do not know why God heaps healing on some and others are seemingly left, weak in the wilderness. It's heartbreaking. It truly is. And honestly, to put our faith on the line to that extreme, we feel exposed right? Then, embarrassed. Alone. Ashamed. But then we wrestle with these words, "Anyone who believes in Him will *never* be put to shame."[58] What do we do with that? Our theology gets tangled.

---

[57] Romans 5:5
[58] Romans 10:11

What I Couldn't See Before

Come what may, I want you to know that you are no fool, you have nothing to be embarrassed about. Your faith is commendable for being so vulnerable.

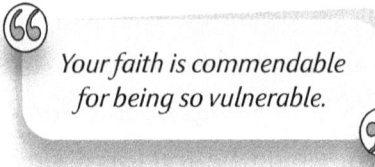
Your faith is commendable for being so vulnerable.

As I dealt with our disappointment, I began to wonder... Could it be that the miracle we're missing is that our faith doesn't fold when our desires are delayed? What if our true testimony to others is not found in the assurance of our ask but rather our response when our request seemingly goes unanswered? What we do with our disappointment can propel us forward or hold us back. Let's not let the enemy win by choosing the latter.

I sheepishly surrendered to injections once again. Unfortunately, RA symptoms were up and running and hostile in my hip. On the bright side, all other joints were contained. But my hip y'all. I remember one night in particular, after returning from the store, it hurt terribly. I decided to try the exercise ball to see if I could stretch it out in hopes to alleviate. This had been going on for a few weeks. I'd tried the R.I.C.E. method consistently: rest, ice, compression and elevation. You guys, nothing was helping. One Saturday, each step brought excruciating pangs. It was so piercing that I was convinced it must be broken, something was terribly wrong. I had Rob drive me to an urgent care facility. Ugh! Nothing was broken. With pain that piercing, I was desperate for a cause, a reason. My reason blew me away. RA. That's it. No injury, nothing else was creating such contention. Truly, it still shocks me at how destructive this disease can be. I left urgent care with a shot and steroids. This stint stretched out over seven long-drawn-out months and 6 doctors! I resonated with the sick woman that bled for twelve years in the Bible: "She had suffered a great deal under the care of many doctors and had spent all she had, yet instead of getting better she grew worse."[59] Can you relate?

I remember being strewn across our bed, pleading, "God, please let this cup pass from me." My quest for relief started with urgent care, then onto my rheumatologist who wanted to just keep me on steroids. I frequented a chiropractor two to three times a week for a couple of months. I saw an alternative pain management doctor who went in and drained fluid from my hip. As you can imagine, our bank account was being drained, too. We then made our way to another doctor who offered prolotherapy, an injection-based treatment to awaken my body's healing properties and attract them to my hip. We tried those multiple times.

In the midst, all dignity depleted, I had to get a temporary handicap sign for parking. That was a pretty low moment, a hard blow, but not as low as what came later. One night after dinner, we were making our way to the car, and I was limping along. Our daughter was five at the time, and with innocent fear in her voice and big, brown eyes, she looked up at me and asked, "Mommy, are you going to heaven soon?" I. WAS. CRUSHED! Not by her words but the raw reality of what she was experiencing. Fighting back tears and my own fears, I sought to reassure her, "Oh baby, Mommy's in a lot of pain. That's all." My heart was so heavy for the weight that she carried.

---

[59] Mark 5:26

What I Couldn't See Before

Chronic pain can lead to chronic depression, and I was headed in that direction. Nothing was helping. I hurt all the time! It hurt to sit, it hurt to walk, it hurt to lie down. I didn't want to live on anti-inflammatories. That's not good for anybody! I saw no end in sight. I was running on E with hope. I always had a fear of dying after abruptly losing my grandmother when I was eight- years-old. I saw her one afternoon, and she was gone that night. It shook my soul, but God used even that for my good. I put my faith in Jesus as my Lord and Savior and was baptized. My eternal future was secured. But the here and now…well, I didn't feel so secure. The pain had been so piercing for so long that I honestly feared it was going to rob me of my finite future with my family. The fear of leaving loved ones too soon broke me. On the other hand, I could not fathom how one could live like this, not knowing when it would end. This terror taunted me, but God would use it to free me. One night, at my lowest of lows, I told the Lord, "Look, I need you to heal me or take me. I can't keep living like this." You can imagine Rob's face the following morning when I informed him of what I told God. He was like, "Do what now?!" BUT, God was moving in that moment of misery. I surrendered my greatest fear to God, and He showed me that there was purpose in my pain. As I sat down to start my daily reading of the Word, I just "randomly" opened my Bible. I wasn't looking for a specific Scripture, but the Scriptures were searching for me. God foreknew that I'd land on Philippians 1:20-25, "I eagerly expect and hope that I will in no way be ashamed but will have sufficient courage so that now as always Christ will be exalted in my body, whether by life or by death. For to me, to live is

> there was purpose in my pain

Christ and to die is gain. If I am to go on living in the body, this will mean fruitful labor for me. Yet what shall I choose? I do not know! I am torn between the two: I desire to depart and be with Christ, which is better by far; BUT IT IS MORE NECESSARY FOR YOU THAT I REMAIN IN THE BODY.

CONVINCED OF THIS, I KNOW THAT I WILL REMAIN, and I will continue with all of you for your progress and joy in the faith." You guys, my page was a puddle. God so precisely told me that I wasn't going anywhere. I surrendered my scare, and He reassured me with His revelation. After reading that, I was convinced that He intended to use this hardship to point others to His Lordship. He Was good! He Is good! He Will be good! I had a newfound fortitude to proverbially "run the race set before me." Would it be easy? No. Would He be with me? Yes

The pain persisted, and we persevered. Life carried on. I got creative with the kids so I could sit and play. We crafted chalk creations in the driveway, and they enjoyed their scooters as I sat, mesmerized at their silliness. Or they'd make their way to the park bench to update me on their adventures while at the playground. Laundry still got loaded and bills still got paid. Rob's PTA was extremely generous and dropped off grocery goodies and readymade meals for a couple of weeks to ease things a bit, and that was a tremendous blessing. I can't fully fathom the burden Rob bore during this time, and I'm so grateful that the PTA was supportive and saw him in the midst of our mess.

Speaking of PTA, another parent came through for us. An orthopedic surgeon, who had a daughter at Rob's school, heard of my situation. He was compelled to move his schedule around to make room for me to see him that week. We were humbled by his willingness to squeeze us in. Humbled, yes. Prepared for what he'd say? No. We explained all the prior doctors we had seen for this situation. He saw the distress in both of us. He informed me that I had more fluid on my hip than a woman in labor. As warm, quiet tears streamed down my face, he told me I needed a hip replacement. A hip replacement. I was thirty-two!

We gave way to a gauntlet of grief. God's grace would sustain us though.

In the meantime, our family was preparing for a colossal change. Caught completely off-guard, Rob was invited to join our church staff team to oversee the Next Gen ministries. Remember how we thought our kids would have their daddy as their principal? Turns out, God had other plans. This was a burn-the-ship moment for Rob. Many worldly leaders in the school district told him he was an idiot if he walked away from retirement pension and the pecking order that he was so prosperously pursuing. But it's a good thing we didn't listen to the world. "Stop deceiving yourselves. If you think you are wise by this world's standards, you need to become a fool to be truly wise. For the wisdom of this world is foolishness to God."[60] Full of insecurities, Rob said yes. We said yes. This invitation was a marker stone moment to remind us that God saw us in our suffering and that this life is not our own. "Whoever tries to keep their life will lose it, and whoever loses their life will preserve it."[61] God didn't just have a plan to preserve our lives, He had plans for us to thrive...even in the throes of our troubles.

We were still saddened by my sad reality. You know, the one where I needed a hip replacement, and I wasn't even near the same

---

[60] 1 Corinthians 3:18,19
[61] Luke 17:33

zip code as being a senior citizen. We wept, but God wouldn't leave us in our woes. Less than a year after moving close to Rob's school, we were now moving to Flower Mound to be close to our church. Guess who came in clutch again? Our amazing young adults that we had the privilege of leading at the time. I was more restricted this go around, and they did nothing but step up their game. From setting up our spice rack to constructing our closet, they dove deep into being the hands and feet that carried us through that move.

Before our significant shift, we had to determine what direction we'd take for my hip. It was May. I had seen six specialists since November. This last doctor said an injection should suffice for the short run, but he thought it MIGHT last til August. "I'll see you in December," he said. He was so sure the shot wouldn't see me any further. Therefore, we scheduled the procedure.

This wasn't a shot in the arm and you're on your way. This required x ray precision for them to pinpoint the place for injection. First, they went in with about 8" of needle full of dye to ensure they'd landed in the joint capsule. Then, they gave me that dose of diversion. It's important to note that these are allowed up to three times per year; hence, the doctor's prediction of their longevity. BUT GOD! You guys, this fix fastened me for five freeing years! My glorious limp had become a walking miracle. We had liberty to live life to its fullest again. So much so, that Rob and I fled to Mexico to carpe diem for an anniversary.

Friend, He has plans for you to thrive in your trial, too. Oftentimes, when and how we least expect it. He is the God who sees you, your El Roi. Will we see Him? Let's not be like the two men on the Walk to Emmaus and miss Jesus right in our midst. His word promises that "You will seek me and find me when you search for me with all your heart."⁶² You know what I was seeking? Healing instead of the Healer. I was so desperate for deliverance, and I was convinced that to be pain free was to live free. And while the pain persisted longer than I liked, He certainly freed me from my fear. I found Him in the Holy love-letter that He's written to us all. He wasn't hiding from me, and He's not hiding from you.

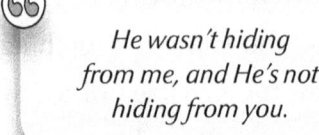

He wasn't hiding from me, and He's not hiding from you.

What are you expending all your energy on instead of sitting with the Great Sustainer? Let's find Jesus in the fractured parts of our story.

---

⁶² Jeremiah 29:13

CHAPTER NINE REFLECTIONS

1. "Everything is possible for one who believes." Mark 9:23
   Is there an area where you think God is calling you to take a Huge leap of faith?
   If so, seek His Word, Godly counsel and unity in that decision. If you're holding back, ask Him to help you trust Him more.

   _____
   _____
   _____
   _____

2. "Hope does not disappoint, because the love of God has been poured out in our hearts by the Holy Spirit, who was given to us." Romans 5:5
   You can bring your disappointment to God when your prayers are not answered the way you hoped. If you haven't ever done so, tell Him your disappointments. He will meet you there.
   Then, ask Him to show you where He was working in the middle of it.

   _____
   _____
   _____
   _____

3. "Everyone around was in awe – all those wonders and signs done through the apostles! And all the believers lived in a wonderful harmony, holding everything in common. They sold whatever they owned and pooled their resources so that each person's need was met." Acts 2:43- 45 MSG

   Take a moment and thank God for those around you that have helped meet your needs.

   _____
   _____
   _____
   _____

   What need can you meet, even in your trial?

   _____
   _____
   _____
   _____

4. "I eagerly expect and hope that I will in no way be ashamed but will have sufficient courage so that now as always Christ will be exalted in my body, whether by life or by death." Philippians 1:20

   How can your current trial give you courage to help others in their greatest time of need?

   _____
   _____
   _____
   _____

Chapter Ten

Humility in Hardship

It was time to take our fractured parts and make them whole.

The waiting room was a traffic jam of walkers, canes or limpers, and any one of them could have been a grandparent, or great-grandparent for that matter. I plodded in there with purpose. It was time to talk about that hip replacement, and we had come to terms with this reality even though I was only thirty-eight.

Initially, we were sedated with sadness. Our someday, now scheduled...for soon. "Doc, can I wait until Fall when our kids are back in school?" I'd like to say that his smile eased the blow, but it didn't, and his answer was 'no.' Surgery was imperative. I saw Rob begin to glaze over as the doctor said I'd be housebound for thirty-plus days, only permitted to get up for thirty minutes at mealtime... on a walker! I quickly, and without hesitation, assured him that we'd be fine. It's not that I had all the answers, but I was confident that our people did. The calls and texts went out as I called on compadres to take charge. With three kids, three dogs, soccer, choir, oh, and don't forget school, we had a lot of ground to cover. Not to mention, I would need someone to help me during the day. AND, dinner! What would we do about meals? Laundry? Groceries?

The need for help is undeniable when you're helpless. Humility and I held hands. My identity was about to be tested. Would insecurity get the victory? Am I loved simply for who I am, not what I do?

Our sadness turned to hope. The doctor assured us that I'd feel like a brand-new person. Permanent relief was on its way, to stay. I so desperately desired to make it to forty before doing this. I was willing to embrace it at forty. I felt like that was a somewhat reasonable time for a hip replacement. It seemed justified. If I could make it to forty, then I would have made it. I was grasping people, grasping. But there would be no more delaying this docket. God's timetable was sooner, and it was time to trust Him. Rob and I had resolve.

Are you at a crossroads where your schedule/outcome doesn't line up with the Lord's? Is it time to stop resisting and trust in His timing? What do you say we stop the wrestling now?

"This left Jacob all alone in the camp, and a man came down and wrestled with him until the dawn began to break."[63]

Friend, what if the dawn is about to break for you? Maybe it's time we stop trying to shove God into our small box of small thinking. We often think we know better, right? He will be God

---

[63] Genesis 32:24

when He heals like . . . answers like . . . We deceptively discern that the only optimal outcome is the one we've constructed. We fit Him into our faith rather than Him forming our faith. I say we bust the box wide open and position ourselves to prosper from the pain, surrendering our will to His. "Now to Him Who is able to do immeasurably more than all we ask or imagine, according to His power that is at work within us."[64] He has so much for us to receive. Don't block the blessing. Jacob got his, and yours is coming.

Let's not allow pity or pouting to prevent us from breakthrough.

It was time to phone a friend, actually several. I remember calling up a group of friends and asking them to meet me for coffee. I gave each of them a small gift card to said coffee shop. I wanted to thank them in advance. I looked at each of them, tears in my eyes, and told them I needed them and would for a while. We were in no position to do this on our own. Jesus didn't want that anyway.

A collective calling would help carry our burden, and we couldn't have been more grateful. "Carry each other's burdens, and in this way you will fulfill the law of Christ."[65]

I would be remiss if I did not mention that my surgery took place the Monday after Easter. I will not let the significance of that slip by. Jesus rose from the dead for our freedom. He conquered death on our behalf. He came for us to live. And we can't forget Lazarus. Mary and Martha sent word to Jesus that their brother

---

[64] Ephesians 3:20
[65] Galatians 6:2

What I Couldn't See Before

was sick. "When He heard this, Jesus said, "This sickness will not end in death. No, it is for God's glory so that God's Son may be glorified through it."[66] "Now Jesus loved Martha and her sister and Lazarus. So, when he heard that Lazarus was sick, he stayed where he was two more days, and then he said, "Let us go back to Judea."[67]

Stayed where He was two more days?! But, Jesus loved them. How does that make any sense? Why didn't He rush to the scene? Run to their rescue? When we lack His penthouse perspective, we can't see His purpose. His ways are higher than our ways, and sometimes that's all we can hang our hat on. God's glory was being primed to be revealed. His disciples proceeded to question Jesus' going back to Judea after already suffering severe persecution. He kindly rebuked them for challenging His call to go, and then He patiently clarified after taking Him literally when He said He was going to wake Lazarus up.

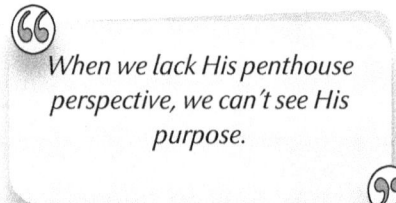

When we lack His penthouse perspective, we can't see His purpose.

"So then He told them plainly, "Lazarus is dead, and for your sake I am glad I was not there, so that you may believe. But let us go to Him."[68] (Do you think Jesus rolled His eyes at them?) Like people, "Have you been walking with Me for any length of time at all? Have you no sense of what I do?!" He was so patient with them, and He's so patient with us.

Lazarus had been dead for four forlorn days. In Jewish culture, it was believed that the spirit could still linger for three

---

[66] John 11:4
[67] John 11:5
[68] John 11:14

days after one's death. Therefore, Jesus was intentionally waiting to raise Lazarus from the dead to assure that others knew he was completely dead. When Martha got word that Jesus was in town, she went to Him in Martha fashion. She essentially scolded Jesus for not having been there when her brother was sick, but she saved her scolding by acknowledging that Jesus could still call on God to do what They do. Mary proceeded to say the same thing to Jesus. Many were there weeping on behalf of their loss. When Jesus saw this, He, too, was moved. In fact, "He wept."[69] Others were starting to stir the pot as some so skeptically do. "But, some of them said, "Could not He Who opened the eyes of the blind man have kept this man from dying?"[70] Jesus made His way to the tomb, and here comes Martha again. She felt the need to give Jesus the heads up that the smell was pungent in there. Jesus puts her in her place by reminding her of Who He is. He opens up in dialogue with His Good Father. Then, Jesus yelled for Lazarus to come out. And the most beautiful words followed, "Take off the grave clothes and let him go."[71] Lazarus was given a new lease on life.

I was about to experience a new life, as well. The old things, gone. New things on the horizon.

A few years before replacements, our lead pastor shared the word "sozo" in a sermon. It means to save,

---

[69] John 11:35
[70] John 11:37
[71] John 11:44

heal and make whole. I had no tattoos at the time, but I knew I wanted that stamped on my body the moment he shared it. Jesus did that for all of us on the cross. He saved, healed and made us whole when He bore all our sin. But, we also get to experience more of that sozo as we are set free from things that have sought to steal, kill and destroy us. I knew what Jesus had done, and I believed there was more. "God, who gives life to the dead and calls those things which do not exist as though they did."[72] Sozo tattooed on my wrist was my way of proclaiming and calling out my body to be whole even though it hadn't yet come to pass.

I was able to share this with my surgeon as he came back before surgery. The doctor prayed over me, and next thing you know, I was out of surgery. Believe it or not, this was done at an outpatient facility. So, I had to get up and walk to the bathroom with my walker in order to pass the test and go home a few hours later. You guys, anesthesia makes me SO sick. Like, super sick! I'll leave it at that. My color was as chalky as well, chalk. Nonetheless, I eventually passed the pee test, and we loaded up to go home.

To have your kids see you in that state is demeaning, to say the least. I summoned a smile as I moseyed in, but my pale complexion was hard to hide. They were gracious, incredible and kind. My parents were there for a few days to help. My friends and our church, that I called on for help, they came in clutch. Our kids had rides to and from school, someone planned to bring us dinner consistently, another friend would take care of our laundry once a week, and another group would do a weekly, grocery run. I was also blessed with the presence of someone every day of the week to bring me lunch and check on me. All defenses were down. Humbled, yes. But

---

[72] Romans 4:17

they all did their darndest to give me my dignity, and that's still sacred space I hold today. I could not help with my hands, but man, my heart was wide open to be with each one as they came to be with me. I still hold onto sweet conversations from that time. Our community became our comfort as we pioneered uncharted territory.

Friend, if we need a hand, we must raise a hand. We're not meant to be self-sufficient, self-reliant, independent beings that trudge through life with piles of problems yet post perfection online. Our vulnerability opens the door. We need each other. The beauty is the variety of ways we can serve. And don't for one minute believe the lie that your act of love is too small or insignificant. Texts are timely, cards are compassionate, and meals are miracles in casserole dishes (or Door Dash passes.) The world needs you, and I needed them. "God is not unjust; He will not forget your work and the love you have shown Him as you have helped His people and continue to help them."[73]

This went on for thirty-three days. I was bedridden except for mealtime. I did not leave the house except for the eventual practice of walking down the sidewalk. Physical therapy was done from the bed for the first two weeks, then I graduated to walking laps around the kitchen. And, you know what?! My hip had NO pain. NO pain!

---

[73] Hebrews 6:10

What I Couldn't See Before

It was gone! G O N E! So, while being confined to the house and bed felt incredibly inconvenient, that's all it was. Persistent pain was no longer permeating there. Rob and I could lay side by side again. The kids and I had sweet snuggles as we'd chat about their day or watch a show together. There was one caveat though. Remember that shoulder replacement that I was told I needed years ago? Well, having to put most of your weight through your arms/shoulders with the walker started to wear on my shoulder again.

Actually, both. I bypassed it and thought it was temporary from the modifications needed.

Excitement arrived on my breakout day from the house. I was stoked to see my surgeon and show him how well I was doing. I even remember playing Michael Buble's song, "Feeling Good" with my daughter and "dancing" with my walker. She smiled as I celebrated. Freedom was in the forecast. If the doctor approved, then I would move on to a cane for two weeks. Then, after that, I'd be footloose and fancy free. I could not have been more ecstatic. Much to our anticipation, I passed with the doctor and promoted to that cane. But he wasn't done. He asked how my shoulder was doing. I told him but also downplayed it a tad. After his assessment though, the symptoms couldn't hide with little range of motion, etc. I could not raise my arm past my chin. He looked at me and said, "Now, it's time to talk about your shoulder."

That was a 1-2 jab that went straight to the gut. What?! Now?! Tears just ran down my face. I told him that I didn't want to be a burden to my husband again, my family. I had felt like a dead weight to them with little to no contribution. He looked at me so intently and said, "This has been your cross to bear, and theirs is to care for you through it."

His closing words though were less than life-giving. He parted with, "When you get tired of being T-Rex, call me."

Yep, that's what he said. Any positive he portrayed went down the chute after that comment. I had not used my left arm much at all for years. We left there with the intent to talk again a few months down the road. I had gone in with such enthusiasm, and I left feeling like my feet had been taken out from under me. Rob, trying to be so positive, offered to take a pic of me with my newfound cane. I wasn't having it! I was pissed not poised. I pouted on the way out, buuuut we bounced back after brunch.

My hip was new, and we were all immensely grateful. Once that two-week window ended, we kicked that cane to the curb and took the dogs for a walk. The kids rode their bikes just ahead of us. The simple, mundane evening was a breath of fresh air to be grateful for. It was now summer, so we enjoyed countless chats at our community pool with friends. We were taking life at a leisurely pace, and things were smooth and low key.

Have you, too found a new appreciation for the little, but in reality, big blessings life has to offer, after going through the fire? It's amazing how our eyes are opened to the goodness of God all around us. That worship song, the bright colors of the bird on your tree, the amazing aroma after rain, the sunset, the wonder of your kids, the servant's heart in others, the ability to linger in conversation and be present. Journeys like these seem to sift out the insignificant. We are enlightened. We now see that the main thing really is the main thing. Am I right with God, and am I right with others? Do

What I Couldn't See Before

my people know Jesus loves and adores them and that I do, too? Am I seeing how I can serve, even if that means sending someone a thoughtful text when bedridden?

Our faith is put under fire, and our circumstances collide with our theology. You start to live life in light of eternity. "Why, you do not even know what will happen tomorrow. What is your life? You are a mist that appears for a little while and then vanishes. Instead, we ought to say, "If it is the Lord's will, we will live and do this or that."[74]

Tough times highlight that the miniscule doesn't matter. The humility of hardship really is a gift. Would I want to repeat the peril? Ummm, no. No, thank you. But I am so very thankful for what I've grasped in the grief. I have an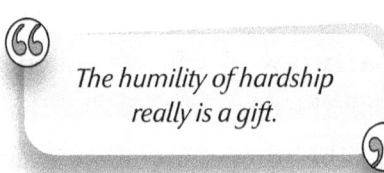

The humility of hardship really is a gift.

appreciation for today, and I am passionate about what people will do with their tomorrow. If you can't yet say you're grateful for this season, can I give you that gentle nudge to simply ask God to show you His good in the midst? It's there, I promise.

He'll lavish you with Kingdom perspective.

Fall came, and more change was coming. At my last hip appointment, I was given an injection for my shoulder. Its longevity was short-lived. We scheduled the shoulder replacement, but with a different doctor this time. We had overcome the hip which gave us hope for this. God affirmed He was with me that day. My

---

[74] James 4:14, 15

surgeon's assistant attended our church. He went with me into surgery, prayed over me and updated Rob post-op. He was a bonus to our breakthrough. It turns out, I had a golf-ball sized, benign cyst just sitting on the top of my shoulder, in addition to RA leaving its mark. I was bound to feel better after getting that thing out. We knew therapy, this go around, would be more challenging. Indeed, it was. I had gone ten, long years with a frozen shoulder, so I had very limited range of motion. I could not raise my arm above my chin that entire time, and we were realistic. I would not get that range of motion back. What's gone was gone. But, silver lining, there's always a silver lining, my therapist was a Jesus-following gal.

She was oh, so great! We hit it off right away. From dry needling to stretching, to heat, to ice and every exercise in between, she spurred me onto stronger. She became a dear friend at that time, and we even kept in touch after I wrapped up that therapy. She was a gem. And the pain was GONE!

Remember how I said that I longed to make it to forty before having these joint replacements? I didn't see the bigger picture. Disappointed I couldn't delay, but on the other side, fiercely relieved. Through it all, I had to choose to trust His timing even though I preferred a different timeline. But you know what?! Spiritual breakthrough happened in December 2018, hip replacement in April 2019 and shoulder replacement in September 2019. What happened six months later? The chaos of COVID! And, two months later, I turned that fabulous forty. Do you see it?

"But do not forget this one thing, dear friends: With the Lord a day is like a thousand years, and a thousand years are like a day. The Lord is not slow in keeping His promise, as some understand

What I Couldn't See Before

slowness. Instead He is patient with you, not wanting anyone to perish, but everyone to come to repentance."[75]

It was the kindness of God to not give me what I wanted in waiting for forty. Had I waited, I would have been denied as it was considered an elective procedure. His timing is trustworthy! He doesn't want us to be destroyed in our darkness. He longs for us to change our mind, change our thinking, our direction... to think His thoughts about our situation, to search for His light in the depths.

Where in your life can you recall the goodness of God now that you're on the other side? What did He spare you from? What did He grant that didn't look like a gift in the moment? He really is incredible and oh so worthy to be trusted.

As I wrap up this chapter, I really am undone that this chapter of life came to a close. My best days were ahead of me and still are. Friend, your best days are ahead! I was so thrilled to mark this moment for His healing, in perfect timing. Sure, we're not immune to other trials but I'm confident that the door had closed on this one. I'm believing and praying the same for you. Let's exit stage right and walk with exuberance knowing we are "clothed with strength and dignity; she can laugh at the days to come."[76]

---

[75] 2 Peter 3:8-9
[76] Proverbs 31:26

CHAPTER TEN REFLECTIONS

1. "Wait for the LORD; be strong and take heart and wait for the LORD." Psalm 27:14

   How do you handle situations where your plans and God's timing do not align?

   _____
   _____
   _____
   _____

2. "Why, you do not even know what will happen tomorrow. What is your life? You are a mist that appears for a little while and then vanishes." James 4:14

   Ask God to help you be aware of what really matters in life and the minutiae that doesn't. Write it down to help keep the proper perspective in place.

   _____
   _____
   _____
   _____

3. "Carry each other's burdens, and in this way you will fulfill the law of Christ." Galatians 6:2

   How can I embrace humility and ask for help from others when I am in need?

   _____
   _____
   _____
   _____

4. "Be devoted to one another in love. Honor one another above yourselves." Romans 12:10
   What is God teaching me about community and the importance of supporting one another?

   _____
   _____
   _____
   _____

5. "I would have lost heart, unless I had believed that I would see the goodness of the Lord in the land of the living." Psalm 27:13
   How have I seen God's goodness in the midst of difficult circumstances?

   _____
   _____
   _____
   _____

Chapter Eleven

Run your Race

I have always dreamed of running a half-marathon. I have such a visual of me crossing the finish line, exhausted and oh so emotional that I did it. I see my family with a sign, cheering me on. I'd run it for me and for them. I'd want to show them that we can do hard things, and when we do, it's beautiful and hard. And worth it. I'm not exactly sure why that's such a dream, but it's one I've longed for, for years. It seems like there would be such a deep-seated satisfaction to have fulfilled such a lofty goal.

I wondered if That could be what I did for my 40th! So, I did my research, talked to a friend and started the process. A new hip, a new shoulder, and I was ready to run! I even went completely vegan for a few months in hopes to position my body for the best possible outcome. I was feeling fantastic. I decided to try one more time to get off RA meds in hopes that maybe I had been holistically healed after my replacements. The stars were aligning. I went for a checkup and bloodwork after being off meds for a couple of months. The next day, I was on a jog, and a call came in from my doctor's office. It was the nurse calling to give me my lab results. I explained to her that I had been jogging, so please forgive my huffs and puffs. She had great news! My numbers were almost undetectable! I was astounded and elated, and the nurse was sharing in my excitement. The doctor knew we were making a run for it again without meds. He thought it worth a shot, too. The nurse cautioned that symptoms could return, but she was genuinely so happy for me.

I had worked my way to mile five, and I was runnin' on cloud nine!

I remember tears just streaming down my face as I ran. Humbled, excited, happy, joyous, thankful, on top of the world. As I ran, I yelled out my gratitude to God. Could it be that RA had been eradicated from my body?! I was incredibly hopeful and wholehearted. Of course I was sore from the training, but I embraced sore. It felt good to be sore again and nothing else. It felt productive and exhilarating, life-giving. I was working towards something.

But six miles would end up being all I could manage. My right knee was starting to swell, insanely bad. I iced, rested, elevated, got a brace and tried to endure and persevere, but it only made matters worse. RA was creeping back, and my knee legitimately had grown to the size of a cantaloupe. No joke. Strangely, it really didn't hurt. It was just terribly, terribly swollen. I was so focused on my dream that I was committed to doing whatever it took to try and get the swelling down.

So, I drank/ate nothing but celery juice for three entire days. That's supposed to be a natural anti-inflammatory. Celery juice, people. Nope, they lied. They were wrong, and my knee was ENORMOUS! By now, we were at the forefront of Covid, and paranoia was pervasive. I placed a call to my doctor, and he said I needed to come in and have my knee drained. Many measures were put in place to carefully be in contact with others. My doctor drained, and drained and drained my knee. He said it was one of the worst he had seen. Instantly, with fluid gone, I freely moved my knee again. Gosh, that felt better. And yea, you guessed it, it wasn't in the cards to do life without meds. We sure tried, didn't we? So, once again, we resumed our regimen. You know what else? I ate a freakin' hamburger! I had been so hopeful that we had concocted the perfect cocktail with a food formula that I dismissed my desires to eat meat. Anything animal related for that matter. But, if I wasn't going to be medicine free, then by all means, I'll savor a steak occasionally.

How I dealt with this disappointment was a miracle. It didn't mangle my mindset. I was able to accept the fact that this just wasn't His will. God was using the medicine to help me stay whole and in a state of healing. But there would be no half-marathon. I was ok with it. I still am. His will be done, not mine. Of course, I was bummed that there would be no monumental mile marker, but I relinquished the fact that my dream didn't align with His for my life.

He has a different race for me to run.

A couple of months later, I had a one-year post op appointment for my hip. X rays were required to see how things had set in place. All looked great, but my left hip, well, the doctor wanted to be the bearer of bad news. He told me I had six months to a year left on that hip. The clock was ticking.

Friend, it still is. Over four years later, and I'm still goin' strong on the original, left hip God gave me. Another miracle! He's the God of possibility! This whole journey has been one monumental mile marker after the other. See what I did there? I've been runnin' my proverbial marathon, and I didn't even realize it. It's just not the race I would've registered for.

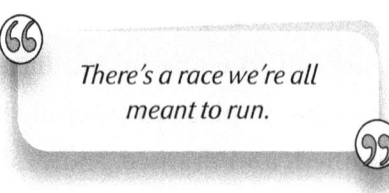
There's a race we're all meant to run.

There's a race we're all meant to run.

"Therefore, since we are surrounded by such a great cloud of witnesses, let us throw off everything that hinders and the sin that so easily entangles. And let us run with perseverance the race marked out for us."[77]

The verses above are meant to spur us on in this spiritual journey, to persist even in pain. God has marked how many miles we'll run in this one life we live. We can't forget, people are watching how we wade thru the weight of this world. Trials are the training ground, and sometimes we go through hell before walking to healing. He doesn't promise pain-free but in fact, the opposite. "In this world you will have trouble. But take heart! I have overcome the world."[78] The Word tells us that we will go from "glory to glory,"[79] and this life can sometimes feel that we go from hardship to hardship. Jerry Bridges said it well in Pursuit of Holiness, "Christianity is an obstacle course of marathon length."

---

[77] Hebrews 12:1
[78] John 16:33
[79] 2 Corinthians 3:18

So, the goal can't be problem-free, but rather to learn how to keep running with endurance when we encounter obstacles.

Life isn't a spiritual sprint.

We're in this for the long haul. Jesus promises, "but the one who stands firm to the end will be saved."[80]

There will be times when we're on cruise control, and we're able to coast. We'll also have peaks of prosperity when we experience the "runner's high." Or, maybe we'll find ourselves limping along and looking for someone to cheer us up and give us sustenance to keep going. Then, there will be seasons when we are crawling and clawing our way through this race. Remember that race.

We can't throw the towel in when our theology is tested and troubles thicken. We run the race set before us and that will come with a gauntlet of emotions.

When life is effortless, it's easy to say we believe in and follow God. But, when the elements start to stretch us, we must remember the reason for the training, why we stay in the Word, why we surround ourselves with saints that will sharpen us, and why we worship because it's warfare.

And, when we feel like we've been kicked in the teeth? Well, we'll wanna quit. We'll start to question why we are running this race to begin with. Is it really worth it? Why would He put you through this? Why do this to yourself? How can this be good?

Friend, don't retreat before your race has been run. Don't take the bait that life will be easier if you exit.

We can't forget that great cloud of witnesses that ran before us. True, some of them didn't see His promises fulfilled this side of

---

[80] Matthew 24:13

heaven, but they didn't quit. Their prize was on eternity. They had the assurance that His promises would play out. "All these people were still living by faith when they died. They did not receive the things promised; they only saw them and welcomed them from a distance, admitting that they were foreigners and strangers on earth."[81]

This is a journey of ultimately trusting God.

Our church holds four core truths that we recite every week:

God is good.

Jesus has forgiven me.

I am loved.

Everything is possible.

Our lead pastor says that it all comes down to these four statements. If there is an area in our lives that we are questioning God and His will for our lives, we can trace it back to doubting one of these truths. It really is that simple.

Which truth are you doubting? More than one? That's ok. There's grace for your doubt. What are your thoughts towards God in your trial?

Do you question His goodness?

Do you strive for forgiveness?

Do you feel unlovable?

Does that thing still seem impossible?

---

[81] Hebrews 11:13

Even now, I have a situation where I struggle to believe these truths in light of my circumstances.

I've found that if we thumb for God thru our trial, then we will be disappointed more times than not. But, if we perceive our problems from God's perspective, then we can take these truths at their word.

Friend, we have to fight the good fight. "For our fight is not against flesh and blood, but against principalities, against powers, against the rulers of the darkness of this world, and against spiritual forces of evil in the heavenly places."[82]

We are at war.

The majority of said war is fought between our thinker and the 12" it travels to our ticker.

The enemy will continuously toss banana peels in our path in hopes to trip us up in our thoughts toward God. He'll drop deceit like,

"How can God be good if He let that happen?"

"He's withholding good things from you."

"No one could ever forgive you for . . ."

"You don't even love yourself, and let me remind you why. So, how could others love you?!"

---

[82] Ephesians 6:12

"If all things were possible, then why are you still single, not pregnant, not healed, still addicted?!"

Satan is only empowered through human agreement.

When we feed on the fruit of his fraudulence, we give him license to keep lying.

The enemy wins when we blame God for our loss, but we must refuse to align our thoughts with the Adversary.

> When we feed on the fruit of his fraudulence, we give him license to keep lying.

Can I plead with you for a moment? God did not cause your catastrophe.

But, there are times when He allows brokenness to lead to our breakthrough.

I'll say it again,

Our suffering is not His fault, and He's not failing when it seems He's not answering.

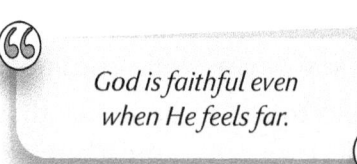

> God is faithful even when He feels far.

God is faithful even when He feels far.

Does this feel too big a pill to swallow? Do you not even want to entertain this thought because you feel so deeply wounded? I 100% understand. Your heart may feel just a little too hard or hurt or both at the moment. I get that. I've been there, and I'm sorry. I'm so, so sorry for your suffering. I've spent much of this journey asking the wrong questions. Maybe you have, too. I have wondered why He allowed it. I have wondered when it will end. What did I do wrong?

Where will this lead? I've wondered if I can trust Him. I've pondered how this could be good. Or, how can I make it stop, make it happen, make it better.

But, I think the main question I missed until recently was who God is to me. May I ask who God is to you? What we think about God will determine how we live our days. I've spent plenty of time doubting the Divine, but He is acquainted with our grief. God sent His one and only Son to die a gruesome death so that we could be in relationship with Him today and spend eternity with Him. "For we do not have a high priest who is unable to sympathize with our weaknesses, but one who in every respect has been tempted as we are, yet without sin."[83]

Jesus, Himself, even asked for the cross to be taken from Him.

But, He drank that cup of agony so that we could live with the assurance that the door on calamity will indeed close.

We may never know why God chooses to heal some this side of heaven and others don't get their miracle until they meet their Maker. The disciples even wanted to know the why, "Rabbi, who sinned, this man or his parents, that he was born blind?" I cherish Jesus' response! "Neither this man nor his parents sinned," said Jesus, "but this happened so that the works of God might be displayed in him."[84]

No one in my family has RA, so it remains a mystery. As my soul has searched for my why or what I did wrong to get RA, those verses have brought so much comfort. It's a natural, human inquiry to want to know why. We long to make sense of it all. You know

---

[83] Hebrews 4:15
[84] John 9:2-3

what happened next in those verses?! Jesus healed the man. "After saying this, He spit on the ground, made some mud with the saliva, and put it on the man's eyes. "Go," He told him, "wash in the Pool of Siloam." "So the man went and washed, and came home seeing."[85]

What if and could it be. . . that our suffering helps us see, like truly see? To see that our trial is temporary even if it lasts our lifetime. "Lord, teach us to number our days, that we may gain a heart of wisdom."[86]

"In all this you greatly rejoice, though now for a little while you may have had to suffer grief in all kinds of trials. These have come so that the proven genuineness of your faith — of greater worth than gold, which perishes even though refined by fire — may result in praise, glory and honor when Jesus Christ is revealed."[87]

Even when Jesus walked this earth, He did not heal or answer to everyone as they saw fit. He healed in different ways, and no two encounters were the same. Remember, He waited to heal Lazarus.

He left Joseph in prison. But, Joseph was later able to confidently say to his brothers after their betrayal, "You intended to harm me,

---

[85] John 9:6-7
[86] Psalm 90:12
[87] 1 Peter 1:6-7

but God intended it for good to accomplish what is now being done, the saving of many lives."[88]

Let's decide that the same will be said of us! David was hiding for his life from Saul in caves. Paul asked many times for the thorn to be taken. The Lord closed Hannah's womb.

Then, the pendulum see-saws the other way. The woman that bled incessantly simply touched His garment, and she was healed. She had been sick for twelve long years!

Jesus healed a man because of his friends' faith. Man, we all need friends like that! Note, Jesus told him, "Son, your sins are forgiven." Jesus restored his relationship with Him before physical breakthrough.

Some were healed by His spoken word. Others, by His touch. There were even times that He healed without even being in the same place as the person in need. Wow!

You'll be happy to hear that Hannah eventually conceived, too.

Oftentimes, God's timing is not our timetable. Joseph? His prison sentence felt permanent at times. But, prison doors opened, shackles removed, and he walked out his purpose. Remember Abraham? He was already elderly

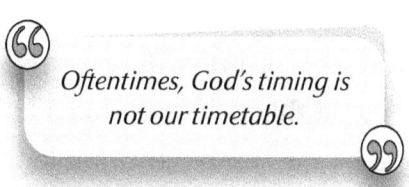
Oftentimes, God's timing is not our timetable.

when God made His promise, and he was much older when it came to pass. Those were laughable circumstances, no doubt. "Abraham fell facedown; he laughed and said to himself, "Will a son be born

---

[88] Genesis 50:20

to a man a hundred years old? Will Sarah bear a child at the age of ninety?"[89]

God's ways our most certainly not our ways. "For my thoughts are not your thoughts, neither are your ways my ways," declares the Lord" "As the heavens are higher than the earth, so are my ways higher than your ways and my thoughts than your thoughts."[90]

We can't forget Job. It seems that Job's job was suffering. Would you agree? Quite literally everything was taken from him, and we see his beautiful, hard wrestle with the Lord over it. God even permitted Satan to afflict Job. "The Lord said to Satan, "Very well, then, he is in your hands; but you must spare his life." "So Satan went out from the presence of the Lord and afflicted Job with painful sores from the soles of his feet to the crown of his head."[91] This affliction was painfully, only the beginning.

We must not forget that God did not cause the affliction but allowed it.

God knew that this was ultimately for Job's good. First, Job was faithful. Then, he was doubtful. He cursed his own birth. Next, resentful. Bitter. Embarrassed. He pled and even pondered why good things happen to bad people and vice versa. We've all asked that question, right? Job longed for the blessings of God's hand to be back in his life. God eventually shows up to the scene in Job 38, and He proceeds to humble Job with His holiness and put Job in his rightful place. My prayer is that our hearts can get to the place where Job's was, after wrestling with God. "Then Job replied to the Lord: "I know that You can do all things; no purpose of Yours

---

[89] Genesis 17:17
[90] Isaiah 55:8-9
[91] Job 2:6-7

can be thwarted. You asked, 'Who is this that obscures my plans without knowledge?' Surely I spoke of things I did not understand, things too wonderful for me to know." "You said, 'Listen now, and I will speak; I will question you, and you shall answer me.' My ears had heard of you but now my eyes have seen you."[92]

There's the seeing again. Job saw what he couldn't see before, as a result of his suffering…things too wonderful for him to know. I pray that we'd receive the same blessing as Job. Now, it may not necessarily be an earthly blessing but rather an eternal perspective while here on this earth. "The Lord blessed the latter part of Job's life more than the former part."[93]

May it be so for us. He promises Heavenly perspective, "I will give you hidden treasures, riches stored in secret places, so that you may know that I am the Lord, the God of Israel, who summons you by name."[94]

Let's find reassurance in the humanity of David as he struggled, as well. The Word of God gives great comfort and reminds us that others have experienced hardship. We are not the exception.

"Be merciful to me, Lord, for I am in distress; my eyes grow weak with sorrow, my soul and body with grief."[95]

---

[92] Job 42:1-5
[93] Job 42:12
[94] Isaiah 45:3
[95] Psalm 31:9

What I Couldn't See Before

"My flesh and my heart may fail, but God is the strength of my heart and my portion forever."[96]

"I cried out to God for help; I cried out to God to hear me. When I was in distress, I sought the Lord; at night I stretched out untiring hands, and I would not be comforted. I remembered you God, and I groaned; I meditated, and my spirit grew faint. Will the Lord reject forever? Will He never show His favor again? Has His unfailing love vanished forever? Has His promise failed for all time? Has God forgotten to be merciful? Has He in anger withheld His compassion?"[97]

In the very same chapter, Psalm 77, David repents. He changes his thinking and what he thinks about God. He, in essence, starts preaching to himself. Let his words be a sermon for your soul today:

> "Then I thought, "To this I will appeal: the years when the Most High stretched out His right hand. I will remember the deeds of the Lord; yes, I will remember Your miracles of long ago. I will consider all Your works and meditate on all Your mighty deeds. Your ways, God, are holy. What god is as great as our God? You are the God who performs miracles; You display Your power among the peoples. With Your mighty arm You redeemed Your people, the descendants of Jacob and Joseph."[98]

David, preach! Preach! In one chapter, he went from weeping to worshipping.

---

[96] Psalm 73:26
[97] Psalm 77:1-3, 7-9
[98] Psalm 77:10-13

God isn't always what we want Him to be, but He's exactly Who we need Him to be. Another big pill to swallow, huh? Forgive me.

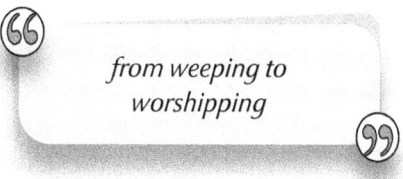
from weeping to worshipping

So, let's go back to my question. Who is God to you?
Do you think He's an angry God?
Distant God?
Punishing God?
Loving Father?
Compassionate Comforter?
Patient Provider?
Loving Leader?

Or, do you expect Him to curate your life like you order your coffee…just to your liking? Ouch! That one stepped on my toes, too. Take a moment to think about the question.

To those of us that have declared God to be our Savior for all of eternity, why on earth would we not trust Him with our suffering today?! I mean, really? It's actually preposterous to think that we have entrusted Him with our eternity, but we struggle to surrender in the here and now.

Job said it so well, "Shall we accept good from God, and not trouble?"[99]

We start to question the goodness of God when things are bad, but who are we to define good? Or bad, for that matter. Honestly. After all that Job endured, he was able to see that God was good all

---

[99] Job 2:10

along. And, I think we can all agree that his circumstances were less than optimal.

God is the standard-bearer for good.

"Give thanks to the Lord, for He is good. His love endures forever."[100]

To my friends that haven't put their faith in Jesus (yet, I hope.) I wish I could lean over my carefully crafted coffee and yours, to say let's run this race together. It's a race worth running. And, heaven and hell? They are both real places where we will spend forever once this life is over. We can get so wrapped up in our physical problems that we forget that the spiritual is superior. "Do not be afraid of those who kill the body but cannot kill the soul. Rather, be afraid of the One who can destroy both soul and body in hell."[101]

Please, please, don't think this life is all there is to live. "Show me, Lord, my life's end and the number of my days; let me know how fleeting my life is. You have made my days a mere handbreadth; the span of my years is as nothing before you. Everyone is but a breath."[102]

So, how would life look differently for you if you believe that God really is good and that He's not the cause of your chaos? If all our hope is in our circumstances, we will be sorely let down time and time again. But, when our hope is in Jesus, we rest in the assurance that this too shall pass. "For everyone born of God

---

[100] Psalm 136:1
[101] Matthew 10:28
[102] Psalm 39:4-5

overcomes the world. This is the victory that has overcome the world, even our faith. Who is it that overcomes the world? Only the one who believes that Jesus is the Son of God."¹⁰³

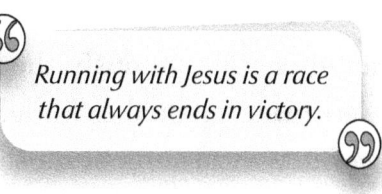

Running with Jesus is a race that always ends in victory.

Running with Jesus is a race that always ends in victory.

And, let me encourage you with who God is if you're still on the fence with your faith. "Praise be to the God and Father of our Lord Jesus Christ, the Father of compassion and the God of all comfort, who comforts us in all our troubles, so that we can comfort those in any trouble with the comfort we ourselves receive from God. For just as we share abundantly in the sufferings of Christ, so also our comfort abounds through Christ."¹⁰⁴

He's a compassionate comforter.

"Don't you see how wonderfully kind, tolerant, and patient God is with you? Does this mean nothing to you? Can't you see that his kindness is intended to turn you from your sin?"¹⁰⁵ Friend, that verse alone reveals His goodness to us. God does not violate our free will. If He did, then He would not be good. But, He's a patient God, and He longs for you to turn towards Him.

Would you pursue Him today in your pain?

---

[103] 1 John 5:4-5
[104] 2 Corinthians 1:3-5
[105] Romans 2:4 NLT

What I Couldn't See Before

C.S. Lewis said, "If we find ourselves with a desire that nothing in this world can satisfy, the most probable explanation is that we were made for another world." You and I, we were made for another world. We will never be satisfied this side of heaven, but man, when we get there...

You see,

"Our final hope is not in our trial ending but in Jesus returning." TVC Podcast

"I consider that our present sufferings are not worth comparing with the glory that will be revealed in us. For in this hope we were saved. But hope that is seen is no hope at all. Who hopes for what they already have? But if we hope for what we do not yet have, we wait for it patiently."[106]

Let this wash over you today, "Though the mountains be shaken and the hills be removed, yet my unfailing love for you will not be shaken nor my covenant of peace be removed," says the Lord, who has compassion on you."[107]

His love never fails, and may His peace pour all over our problems.

Let Jesus see and love you in the very midst of your trembling troubles.

As I reflect back on each mile marker of my journey, I have a confession.

I now see what I couldn't see before.

---

[106] Romans 8:18, 24-25
[107] Isaiah 54:10

I see the goodness of God.

In the thick of it, I couldn't see His hand, Hear His voice, feel His presence. I had glimpses, but, my vantage point was skewed. It often can be in the midst of pain. I can now see He was there all along, that His timing was timely, that He didn't abandon, betray or turn His back on me. I can now see that He's trustworthy and truly does work all things for my good.

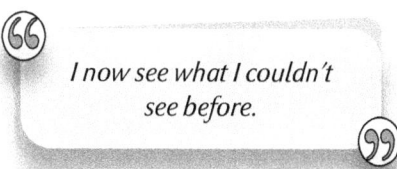

I now see what I couldn't see before.

I wonder, what could you not see before? Ask God to show you.

"And we boast in the hope of the glory of God. Not only so, but we also glory in our sufferings, because we know that suffering produces perseverance; perseverance, character; and character, hope. And hope does not put us to shame, because God's love has been poured out into our hearts through the Holy Spirit, who has been given to us."[108]

I've accumulated 12 inches of scars. Each incision has carried its own story. Your scars, seen or unseen, tell a story, too.

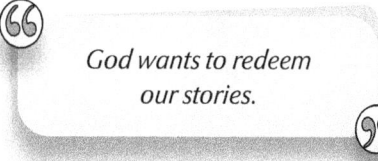

God wants to redeem our stories.

---

[108] Romans 5:2b-5

What I Couldn't See Before

We often create our own script in the suffering in order to cope. But, God wants to redeem our stories.

I still have rheumatoid arthritis. I still take two different medications and six injections a month. I still have two crooked toes that are marker stones of where we've been. I still can't raise my arm above my chin nor will I this side of heaven. I've had two joint replacements, and you'll still find me wearing wrist splints on occasion. It all tells a story.

For years, the story I told myself was that it was my fault. It was my fault I was sexually assaulted. It was my fault I got RA. I no longer believe those things are my fault. I was unaware that I was battling self-hatred, and I didn't even realize the toll my thoughts were taking on my soul. I paid a price in believing those lies. The enemy crept in with lies, but I refuse to give him all the credit. I must own my part with grace. His lies became self-talk. Now, I talk back to him whenever he attempts to tangle me up. I'm a beloved daughter in whom God is well pleased. I am worthy and a part of God's royal priesthood.

I have learned self-compassion. Show yourself some, too. We didn't know what we didn't know. That's ok. I have learned that God is not up there shaking His finger at me in utter disgust. I have learned that He has grieved alongside me in my pain. I have learned that joy and sorrow can coexist. I have learned to let others in. I hope you can let others do the same for you.

Having community to help carry your burdens is a gift and necessary to sustain you in your suffering.

God has transformed my brokenness into breakthrough.

I did not cause RA, and neither did God. We live in a broken world, but God has transformed my brokenness into breakthrough.

There has been a 6th stage of grieving that's been added to the former five stages: denial, anger, bargaining, depression and acceptance. The 6th stage is purpose.

He's brought purpose to my pain and clarity to my calling. Don't let your pain be pointless.

> *He's brought purpose to my pain and clarity to my calling. Don't let your pain be pointless.*

I've learned to receive His grace, I've experienced His presence, and now we get to partner with Him in our pain. If we find purpose, then it provides perseverance. I long to carry hope to the hopeless, to see you in your hurt. "And we know that in all things God works for the good of those who love him, who have been called according to His purpose."[109]

I may never know why I have RA, but I don't need to anymore. What if we ask a different question? God, have you entrusted me with this to point others to You? I pray that He can use the years of pain like God used Paul's: "Now I want you to know, brothers and sisters, that what has happened to me has actually advanced the gospel..."[110]

"And so, dear brothers and sisters, I plead with you to give your bodies to God because of all he has done for you. Let them be a living and holy sacrifice—the kind he will find acceptable. This is truly the way to worship him."[111]

---

[109] Romans 8:28
[110] Philippians 1:12
[111] Romans 12:1 NLT

God can use our hard for healing when we share our stories with others.

In the very midst of writing this book, I was diagnosed with a congenital heart abnormality. One test called for another, and I prayed for a miracle. I prayed that the next test would reveal a mistake and the first test misread. It wasn't. Abnormality confirmed. I went in full of faith. Now, after that diagnosis, I dealt with disappointment, again. I wept but only for a moment. I have prayed for more faith to believe that He fearfully and wonderfully made me that way, on purpose. Simultaneously, my husband was diagnosed with a spot of melanoma, but praise God they caught it early and margins are clear now.

Hardship to hardship sometimes, right? But, BUT, in it all,

"I remain confident of this: I will see the goodness of the LORD in the land of the living."[110]

I HAVE seen the goodness of God in the land of the living. My husband has been the steady in the storm, the pure embodiment of Jesus. I have learned such a deep appreciation of life and its true meaning that I know only my trials have taught me. I pursue our kids' hearts with passion because I long for them to know that God is good and He's good to them. I'm grateful for what hard has helped me to see. I remember saying to my husband, when our kids were very young, that even though the early years have been rough, I was confident that better days were ahead.

Fast forward to last year, my daughter and I went to a high school girls' conference together.

That weekend, the Lord illuminated this verse,

"I will repay you for the years the locusts have eaten."[112]

    I paused, I sat and stared at that Scripture. I swallowed the lump in my throat, I let the tears fall, I looked my daughter in the eye, I told her how grateful I was for her and that moment, and we stood, side by side and worshipped our good God together. This moment, this milestone marker, became a stone of remembrance for us. We enjoyed God's faithfulness - together. This was a moment for her to see that He is good to her.

    I want to share another mile marker moment with you. While writing this, I attended a local women's conference that I was invited to by a friend. With the fullness of life, I questioned if this was my "best yes." On the last day, the speaker shared that each woman attending was prayed for before the conference began. The table leaders had a sealed envelope for each lovely lady at their table. These people did not know me. It was a Holy moment. A moment that solidified the suffering. A moment that felt like Jesus and I were on my comfy couch, and He handed me a gift that He'd been waiting for so long to hand me. It's like He was the kid on Christmas morning, so eager for me to open it. Inside the sealed envelope, I read these words,

---

[112] Psalm 27:13

STEADFAST LOVE

"Who redeems your life from the pit, who crowns you with steadfast love and mercy."[113]

"Your love for God is a steadfast love. You have walked through the fire, near death, but He pulled you out of the pit. You went from death to life. Your love for Him is firm and unwavering. Unshakable. This love is not out of duty but out of desire because of what He has done for you. He pulled you out and you fully trust that He is faithful. You have come to know that His love will not disappoint. In His loving kindness, I hear Him calling you to step out and help pull those out of the pit. Do not worry, He will sure as not even let your foot slip, His love for you is firm, unwavering and unshakable. And He desires to redeem it all! It is for freedom that Christ has set us free."

I wish I could add crying emojis here. Beauty from ashes, friends. Beauty from ashes. Can you believe it?! I was literally undone at His kindness to me in those words. The revelation of purpose in the pain. You better believe His Word is living and active!

Did you catch it? I now have the humble privilege to help pull you out of your pit.

We learn to dance with the belief that our healing can still come in the here and now and knowing it will come in the then and there. So, yes, I still have RA, and yes, I have been healed. Yes and yes. My

---

[113] Psalms 103:4 ESV

heart is whole now. My perspective has changed. I have limitations, but I embrace what I *can* do. Speaking of, it's time to walk my dogs. My four-legged Hope carriers that have been with me through it all, my therapy. In the beautiful wrestle, God has healed my heart, and He's used modern medicine to help in my physical healing.

I have fought for my faith, and I pray this can be said of you and me, "He said to her, "Daughter, your faith has healed you. Go in peace and be freed from your suffering."[114]

So, what do you say? Let's run our races together. I'm cheering you on, and more importantly, so is Jesus. As you run your race, picture Jesus and the sign He's holding up, "I believe in you. I'm so proud of you. Keep going. Don't quit. You're brave. You're doing awesome! Crossing that finish line will be worth it."

And then, when He sees us struggling, and we fear our feet can't go any further, He'll break through the barricade, come for us and start running alongside us. He's running towards you and with you.

Friend, it has been an honor to walk with you through these pages, and I hope you have felt a friend holding your hand as you have. I pray you've found Hope for your heart and your hurt, and I want to leave you with one final statement. I pray you come to believe it in your bones. It changes everything!

God's not holding out on you, He's holding onto you.

---

[114] Mark 5:34

CHAPTER ELEVEN REFLECTIONS

1. "Let us run with perseverance the race marked out for us." Hebrews 12:1

   What dreams or goals have you pursued that required perseverance and faith?

   _____
   _____
   _____
   _____

2. "I will restore you to health and heal your wounds,' declares the Lord." Jeremiah 30:17

   In what ways have you experienced healing or hope despite challenges?

   _____
   _____
   _____
   _____

3. "For no matter how many promises God has made, they are 'Yes' in Christ." 2 Corinthians 1:20

   Which truths about God have you embraced that have strengthened your faith?

   _____
   _____
   _____
   _____

"God is good. Jesus has forgiven me. I am loved. Everything is possible."

_____
_____
_____
_____

4. "But what about you?" he asked. "Who do you say I am?" Mark 8:29

    Remember, one of the most important questions you must answer is who God is to you. It will impact every area of your life. Who is God to you?

_____
_____
_____
_____

Take time to explore what the Bible says about Who God is.

_____
_____
_____
_____

5. "Then their eyes were opened and they recognized him. They asked each other, "Were not our hearts burning within us while he talked with us on the road and opened the Scriptures to us?" Luke 24:31

   What situation have you been asking God, "why?"

   _____
   _____
   _____
   _____

   Instead, ask Him to show you what you couldn't see before.

   _____
   _____
   _____
   _____

Acknowledgments

Thank You, Lord, for showing me what I couldn't see before... that You never left and You never will.

Rob, I love you. We share something significant because of the suffering. By the grace of God, we have turned inward in the hard and that doesn't always happen. I'm thankful we have partnered through the pain. Let's keep partnering as we walk out His promises for us. Here's to hiking to higher places together. And, thank you for tolerating my over-dramatized feelings of seeing this to fruition. You're a saint.

Harleigh and Sterling, thank you for making me a better human. Thank you for giving me the confidence to write this book. Thank you for being your fearfully and wonderfully made selves, each a genius in your own right. I love watching you learn to run in your lane for Jesus. A doctor once told me that I should have treated my RA non-stop and not paused for childbearing years. Then, he looked at me and said, "But, I guess you're glad you had kids." Ummm, 1000%! I'd do it all over again if it meant we got you at the end! You inspire me, and I couldn't be more grateful to share this life with you. We are immensely proud of who you are and who you're becoming.

What I Couldn't See Before

Walls have come down, barriers broken, roots revealed, lies replaced with Truth, generational curses ceased...all so our ceiling can be your floor.

Callen, you are a beloved son. God is good. And, I'm excited for you to grow in perceiving His goodness and how loved you are. You are resilient, and everything is possible. You have an unbelievable ability to memorize, and that blows us all away. God has blessed you with a brilliant mind, and we look forward to seeing how God uses you for His glory. The best is yet to come, your passions keep changing and growing, and we hope you grow in your passion for Jesus. He is oh so passionate about you!

Mom and Dad, thank you for loving me through it all. Thank you for your friendship. Thank you for entrusting me to God when I wallowed in the world. I pray this book honors you for not giving up on me. I love you.

To April, you have honestly been through it All with me. You were at the hospital before we were for the birth of Harleigh and beat us to the surgery center before my hip replacement. You are the most loyal person I know. Life doesn't allow us facetime as often as we'd like, but our quarterly breakfasts have been a balm to my bruised heart many times. I love you. Thank you.

Pastor John and Colleen, you have loved and led Valley Creek Church with such sacrifice. Thank you for continuing to say "yes" to Jesus and this church family you've found in Texas. Thank you for persevering, enduring, and pressing through the hard for the good of others and the glory of God. Thank you for all the heartwork you've done to teach us the Father's heart. Sitting under your teaching for almost 20 years has changed my life and taught me how to live free. You have been instrumental in my healing journey.

Thank you! Thank you for the freedom to run in my lane for Jesus wherever He's calling me. I pray this book lets you feast on the fruit of your labor for all the years of your leadership. We are incredibly grateful for who you are and that we get to be family on mission. Here's to doing it a long time…together!

To those that said, "Hey, you should write a book." Thank you. You planted the seed. I was reluctant, but God confirmed it and made it grow. Thank you to any and everyone that supported me through the process. No text was too small and your encouragement was timely. Thank you to those that supported my publishing process. We are so very thankful. Thank you to the prayer team that interceded over these pages as I poured out my heart. You helped me keep going. We could not have done this without you.

To Don and Suzanne Manning and Crazy Cool Family, you awakened the writing muscle that had atrophied. Thank you for entrusting me for a season and for supporting this endeavor.

To Jacquetta, my patient publisher, thank you for believing in this story for God's glory. Thank you for bringing it to life. Thank you for being so incredibly patient with this tech-deficient girl in the process. Thank you for hearing my heart throughout and for not settling. It's been a pleasure to work together.

Finally, to Valley Creek Church, thank you for so tenderly stewarding my heart through the suffering. Thank you that I could come as I was, and you loved me still. Thank you for being home through it all. We are forever changed by your friendship, support, love and community. There's always more with Jesus, and here's to our best days ahead!

"However, I consider my life worth nothing to me; my only aim is to finish the race and complete the task the Lord Jesus has given me – the task of testifying to the good news of God's grace."

-Acts 20:24

www.ingramcontent.com/pod-product-compliance
Lightning Source LLC
Chambersburg PA
CBHW070148100426
42743CB00013B/2845